Home for the Harvest

by Nancy Smith & Lynda Milligan

☆ ☆ ☆ ☆ ☆
POSSIBILITIES®
…Publishers of DreamSpinners® patterns, I'll Teach
Myself™ sewing products, and Possibilities® books…

Acknowledgements

We would like to dedicate this book to our very good friend and longtime employee, Jane Dumler.

Jane was recruited early on—about 18 years ago—by Lynda to help out in the shop. She is still helping out! Jane is a pattern drafter/designer in the design part of our business. She also designs and sews custom riding clothes for her home-based business, H.C. Designs. Her sewing and patchwork skills have been greatly appreciated by us over the years. She is a quilting teacher in our shop as well and has won our "most patience" award on more than one occasion. At quilt markets and in our shop, Jane has very successfully taught our *I'll Teach Myself*® sewing program to children.

Jane often refers to herself as Old Mother Dumler, and we are very happy to have had long association with Old Mother Dumler!

Thank you, Jane!

Lynda & Nancy

Special Thanks

Jane Dumler, Joanne Malone, Jan Hagan, Ann Petersen,
Michelle Schlichenmayer, Courtenay Hughes — Stitching
Carolyn Schmitt, Sandi Fruehling, & Susan F. Geddes — Long-arm machine quilting
Blue Rabbit, Ltd., 5210 E. Arapahoe Rd., Littleton, CO 80122   303-843-9419 — Photography in their shop
Country Stencils, 9510 Daybreak Dr., Knoxville, TN 37931   423-769-3887 — Stencils & pillows
The Great Frame Up 7533 S. University, Littleton, CO 80122   303-794-3575 — Framing
South Seas Imports, Westfalenstoffe, & Peter Pan Fabrics — Fabric collections
Ashley Smith Lawler — Photography in her home

Credits

Sharon Holmes — Editor, Technical Illustrator
Sara Tuttle — Hand Illustrator, Designer
Susan Johnson — Designer, Photo Stylist
Valerie Perrone — Designer
Debbe Linn — Technical Illustrator
Chris Scott — Editorial Assistant
Sandi Fruehling — Copy Reader
Brian Birlauf — Photographer

Cynthia Keim Miller
37742 Sodaville Cutoff
Lebanon, OR 97355

…Publishers of DreamSpinners® patterns, I'll Teach Myself™ sewing products, and Possibilities® books…

Home for the Harvest

Published in the United States of America by Possibilities®, Denver, Colorado.
Library of Congress Catalog Card Number: 00-101817
ISBN: 1-880972-41-7

Photo Index

ENLARGING PATTERNS We try to fill our books with as many projects as possible. Because of this, some patterns may have to be enlarged on a copier or with a home computer/scanner setup. We know this may be an inconvenience, but we are sure you will be delighted with your finished project.

APPLIQUE Our favorite method of applique is the fusible web technique with a buttonhole stitch finish. Patterns are reversed and ready to be traced. Be sure to have plenty of fusible web on hand if using this method. Add seam allowance to patterns if doing hand applique.

Little Witch

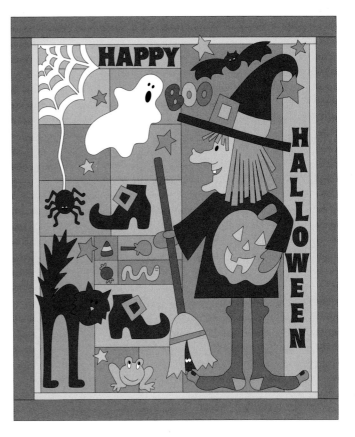

Photo on page 17

SMALL VERSION: Approximate size 24x29″

Use 42-44″-wide fabric. When strips appear in the cutting list, cut crossgrain strips (selvage to selvage).

Yardage

Backgrounds	see cutting chart below
Appliques	large scraps – up to 12″ square
Border 1	⅙ yd.
Border 2	¼ yd.
Backing	⅞ yd.
Binding	⅓ yd.
Batting	28x33″

Cutting Patterns on pages 34-38

Backgrounds – measurements are given width by height and include seam allowance

1 – witch	8 x 25½″
2 – lettering at right	2½ x 25½″
3 – lettering at top	11 x 2¼″
4 – spiderweb	5¾ x 4½″
5 – ghost	5¾ x 4½″
6 – spider tether	5¾ x 4½″
7 – ghost	5¾ x 4½″
8 – spider	5¾ x 4½″
9 – boot	5¾ x 4½″
10 – cat	4½ x 11¾″
11 – candy corn	2¼ x 2¼″
12 – candy	2¼ x 2¼″
13 – sucker	5¼ x 2¼″
14 – worm	5¼ x 2¼″
15 – boot	7 x 5″
16 – frog	3¾ x 3¾″
17 – broom	3¾ x 3¾″

Appliques — Use photo & whole-quilt diagram as guides. Cut one broom handle ⅝ x 12″.

Border 1	3 strips 1″ wide
Border 2	3 strips 2″ wide
Binding	3 strips 2½″ wide

Directions

Use ¼″ seam allowance unless otherwise noted.

1. Stitch backgrounds together following diagram. The dimensions of the backgrounds in the cutting chart are given width first to clarify how they fit into the quilt layout.

2. Border 1: Measure length of quilt. Piece border strips to the measured length and stitch to sides of quilt. Repeat at top and bottom. Press.

3. Border 2: Repeat Step 2.

4. Applique quilt using your favorite method. Our favorite method is fusible web, and our patterns are set up for it—reversed for tracing and no seam allowances added. Cut dress sleeve on gray lines as indicated on pattern. Slip pumpkin under sleeve and hand.

5. Layer top with backing and batting. Quilt. Trim backing and batting even with top.

6. Stitch binding strips together end to end. Press in half lengthwise, wrong sides together. Bind quilt using ⅜″ seam allowance.

1.

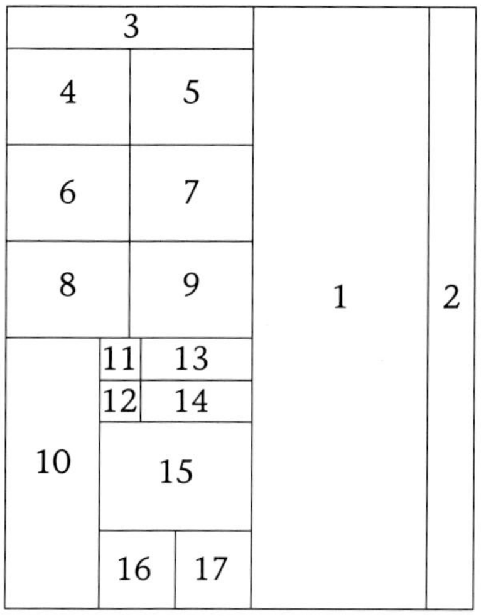

```
┌─────────────────────┬──────┬────┐
│          3          │      │    │
├──────────┬──────────┤      │    │
│    4     │    5     │      │    │
├──────────┼──────────┤      │    │
│    6     │    7     │      │    │
├──────────┼──────────┤  1   │ 2  │
│    8     │    9     │      │    │
├─────┬────┼──────────┤      │    │
│     │ 11 │ 13       │      │    │
│     ├────┼──────────┤      │    │
│ 10  │ 12 │ 14       │      │    │
│     ├────┴──────────┤      │    │
│     │     15        │      │    │
├─────┼─────┬─────────┤      │    │
│     │ 16  │   17    │      │    │
└─────┴─────┴─────────┴──────┴────┘
```

Little Witch

LARGE VERSION: Approximate size 34x41″

Some readers of one of our recent books called to say they had trouble enlarging our patterns, so we made Little Witch in the largest size possible with patterns that fit on our pages. However, for those of you who are able to enlarge patterns and don't mind doing it, we give you this alternate version of Little Witch. Have fun!

NOTE: This version of the quilt requires 140% photocopies to be made of the applique patterns. See notes on pattern pages.

Use 42-44″-wide fabric. When strips appear in the cutting list, cut crossgrain strips (selvage to selvage).

Yardage

Backgrounds	see cutting chart at right
Appliques	large scraps – up to 17″ square
Border 1	¼ yd.
Border 2	½ yd.
Backing	1½ yds.
Binding	⅜ yd.
Batting	38x45″

Cutting Patterns on pages 34-38

Backgrounds – measurements are given width by height and include seam allowance

1 – witch	11 x 35½″
2 – lettering at right	3⅜ x 35½″
3 – lettering at top	15¼ x 3″
4 – spiderweb	7⅞ x 6⅛″
5 – ghost	7⅞ x 6⅛″
6 – spider tether	7⅞ x 6⅛″
7 – ghost	7⅞ x 6⅛″
8 – spider	7⅞ x 6⅛″
9 – boot	7⅞ x 6⅛″
10 – cat	6 x 16⅛″
11 – candy corn	3 x 3″
12 – candy	3 x 3″
13 – sucker	7¼ x 3″
14 – worm	7¼ x 3″
15 – boot	9¾ x 6½″
16 – frog	5⅛ x 5⅛″
17 – broom	5⅛ x 5⅛″

Appliques Use photo & whole-quilt diagram as guides. Cut one broom handle ⅞ x 17″.

Border 1	4 strips 1¼″ wide
Border 2	4 strips 2¾″ wide
Binding	4 strips 2½″ wide

Directions

Follow Steps 1-6 on pages 4 and 5.

Country Spice

Photo on page 20

Approximate size 53x64″

8″ blocks set on point – 32 blocks

Use 42-44″-wide fabric. When strips appear in the cutting list, cut crossgrain strips (selvage to selvage).

NOTE: The yardage listed, 16 fabrics, makes a quilt with minimum waste. Adding more fabrics will make the quilt more scrappy. Our sample was made with 64 scrap fabrics.

Yardage

Blocks, setting triangles, borders, binding
  ½ yd. each of 16 fabrics – half medium to light, half medium to dark
Backing   3½ yds.
Batting   59x70″

Cutting

Cut from each half yard, referring to diagram:
  Borders & binding – 3 rectangles 2½x18″
  Large block triangles – 2 squares 6⅞″
  Small block triangles – 14 squares 2⅞″
  Side setting triangles – 1 rectangle 6⅜x12⅝″

Cut from 4 of the half yards, referring to diagram:
  Corner setting triangles – 1 square 6½″

Directions

Use ¼″ seam allowance unless otherwise noted.

1. Cut the squares for the large block triangles, the small block triangles, and the corner setting triangles in half diagonally.

2. Fold the rectangles for the side setting triangles in half as shown. Cut in half diagonally.

3. Make 32 blocks with 2 fabrics each, as shown. NOTE: If using 16 fabrics, each fabric appears in four blocks. Press.

4. Lay out blocks and setting triangles in diagonal rows. Stitch each row of blocks and setting triangles together.

5. Stitch rows together. Press.

6. Cut border strips into unequal lengths if desired. Stitch together end to end to fit sides of

quilt. Stitch borders to sides of quilt. Repeat at top and bottom. Repeat for a second border.

7. Piece backing horizontally to same size as batting. Layer and quilt. Trim backing and batting even with top.

8. Stitch remaining 18″ strips together end to end. Press in half lengthwise, wrong sides together. Bind quilt using ⅜″ seam allowance.

1.

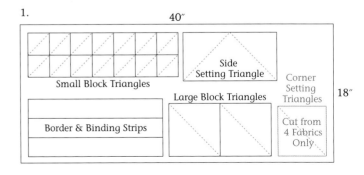

40″

Small Block Triangles

Side Setting Triangle

Large Block Triangles

Corner Setting Triangles

Cut from 4 Fabrics Only

Border & Binding Strips

18″

2.

Fold Cut

Side
Setting Triangle

4.

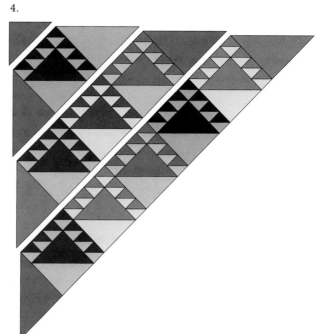

3.

For 1 Block

 Make 7

Make 1

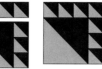

Make 1

Make 1

Pumpkin Cookies with Penuche Frosting

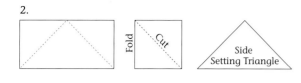

1 cup shortening	1 tsp soda	Penuche Frosting:
½ cup brown sugar	1 tsp baking powder	3 tbsp butter
½ cup granulated sugar	1 tsp cinnamon	½ cup brown sugar
1 cup canned pumpkin	½ tsp salt	¼ cup milk
1 egg	1 cup chopped nuts	2 cups powdered
1 tsp vanilla	1 cup raisins (optional)	sugar (approx.)
2 cups + 2 tbsp flour		

Cream shortening and sugars. Add pumpkin, egg, and vanilla. Mix well. Sift together flour, soda, baking powder, cinnamon, and salt. Add to creamed mixture. Add nuts and raisins. Drop from teaspoon onto ungreased baking sheet. Bake 10-12 minutes at 350˚. Cool. Ice with penuche frosting. Makes 5-6 dozen.

Penuche Frosting: Combine butter and sugar and bring to a boil. Cook and stir about one minute or until slightly thickened. Cool 15 minutes. Add milk and beat until smooth. Add enough powdered sugar for spreading consistency.

Harvest Scarecrow

Photos on pages 21, 24, 49, 52, 57, 64

Approximate height 27″

Materials

Body/head – muslin	⅜ yd.
Pants	⅞ yd.
Shirt	¾ yd.
Hat	½ yd.
Kerchief	⅝ yd.
Fusible interfacing for hat	⅝ yd.
Fiberfill	1 lb.
Nose & cheeks	scraps
Buttons for eyes (optional)	2 – about 1″
Raffia – natural	1 pkg.
Jute	2-3 yds.
Single-fold bias tape to match shirt fabric	¾ yd.

Embroidery floss or permanent marking pen

Cutting Patterns on pages 40-41

Body/head	2
Pants	2 rectangles – 18x24″
Shirt	1 rectangle – 34x24″
Hat	2 crowns
	2 brims on fold
Kerchief	1 square – 18″

Directions

Use ¼″ seam allowance unless otherwise noted.

BODY/HEAD

1. Mark face on front body piece. Place body/head pieces right sides together. Stitch around body/head, leaving bottom edge open for stuffing. Clip and turn right side out. Stuff firmly and stitch bottom edge closed.

2. Face: Nose and cheeks can be fabric pieces attached to face with fusible web, or they can be hand stitched with embroidery floss. Embroider or penstitch mouth, eyes, and brows. Button eyes are also an option.

HANDS & FEET

1. Make 4 bunches of raffia approximately 1″ in diameter.

SHIRT

1. Fold 34x24″ rectangle in half lengthwise and then crosswise to make a rectangle 17x12″.

2. Using diagram, mark and cut neckline and underarm lines.

3. For facing/ casing, stitch bias tape along neck edge, right sides together. Fold to inside and stitch close to fold.

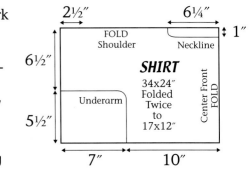

4. Stitch underarm seams. Clip and turn right side out. Press ¼″ to wrong side and stitch in place for sleeve hems.

5. Insert a bundle of raffia at each wrist. Tie a piece of jute tightly around sleeve to hold the raffia in place.

6. Stuff sleeves loosely with fiberfill.

7. Put shirt on body. Using a large blunt needle, thread jute through bias casing at center front. Enter and exit on right side of shirt. Pull tight to fit neck. Tie in a bow or knot and let ends hang.

PANTS

1. Mark and cut inseam on each piece 11″ from bottom edge.

2. Place pants pieces right sides together and stitch side seams.

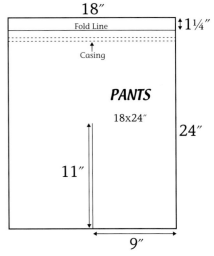

8

3. Casing: Press top edge of pants 1¼" to wrong side. Stitch ¼" from raw edge and again ¼" away to form casing.

4. Stitch inseam. Clip. Turn pants right side out. Press ¼" to wrong side at each cuff and stitch in place.

5. Using a large blunt needle and 42" piece of jute, thread jute through casing. Enter and exit on right side of pants at center front.

6. Insert a bundle of raffia into each leg. Tie a piece of jute tightly around leg to hold the raffia in place.

7. Stuff pants legs loosely with fiberfill.

8. Pull pants on body over shirt. Pull up jute to fit waist tightly. Tie jute in bow and let ends hang.

HAT

1. Apply fusible interfacing to wrong sides of both crowns and both brims.

2. Stitch crown pieces right sides together, leaving bottom open. Trim seam; clip curves; turn.

3. Stitch short seam of each brim piece, right sides together. Trim seam and press open. Lay brim pieces wrong sides together and pin. Topstitch brim pieces, wrong sides together, ¼" from long curvy edge.

4. Pin brim to crown, matching back seams of brim to center back of crown. Stitch. Press seam toward crown.

5. Put hat on scarecrow. Push small bunches of raffia under hat at edge of head. Trim to desired length. Pull hat down until it fits snugly.

KERCHIEF

Fold square in half, wrong sides together, and tie around scarecrow's neck.

OPTIONAL SUSPENDERS

1. Cut two 3½x18" pieces of pants fabric. Fold each in half lengthwise, right sides together. Stitch long side. Turn right side out. Press.

2. Stitch to pants with ⅞" buttons on outside and ends of suspenders on inside.

Leaf Wreath

Photo on page 57. Diameter 18".

Materials

Leaves	1 yd. each of 9 fabrics
Fusible web	10¼ yds.
Straw wreath	14" diameter
Template plastic	9" square
Tacky fabric glue	
Wooden chopstick or Phillips screwdriver	
Purchased wire wreath hanger	

Directions

1. Make plastic template from pattern on page 42.

2. Cut fusible web into nine 17x40" pieces.

3. Make "double fabric": Following manufacturer's directions, bond fusible web piece to wrong side of one leaf fabric (17" sides of web parallel with selvages, 40" side even with cut edge). Peel away paper backing. Fold over the other half of the fabric and bond. One yard of fabric becomes one-half yard of "double fabric". Repeat with other 8 fabrics.

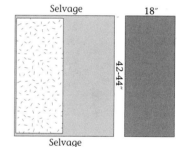

4. Trace around template 10 times on each fabric for a total of 90 leaf units. Cut out.

5. Place end of chopstick or screwdriver in center of one leaf unit where all the stems meet. Hold leaves around chopstick, dip into glue, and push into wreath up to edges of leaves. Twist leaves to make them stand up and away from each other. Make one straight row on outside curve of wreath with approximately 24 leaf units, one straight row on inside curve with approximately 14 leaf units, and two staggered rows along top, placing leaf units 1½-2" apart.

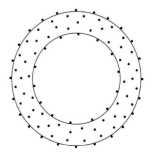

6. Attach hanger.

Indian Summer

Photo on page 24

Approximate size 72x90″

9″ blocks set 8x10

Use 42-44″-wide fabric. When strips appear in the cutting list, cut crossgrain strips (selvage to selvage).

Yardage

Background 1	1 yd. – Block A
Background 2	1 yd. – Block A
Background 3	1 yd. – Block A
Background 4	1¼ yds. – Block B
Purple print	1½ yds.
Rust print	2⅛ yds.
Green print	1 yd.
Backing	5⅝ yds.
Binding	¾ yd.
Batting	78x96″

Cutting

Backgrounds 1-3
Block A   48 rectangles each – 3¾x5⅝″
Background 4
Block B   48 squares – 5⅜″
Purple print
Block A   48 rectangles each – 3¾x5⅝″
Block B   16 squares – 5⅜″
Rust print
Block A   48 rectangles each – 3¾x5⅝″
Block B   16 squares – 9⅞″
Green print
Block A   48 rectangles each – 3¾x5⅝″
Binding   9 strips 2½″ wide

Directions

Use ¼″ seam allowance unless otherwise noted.

1. Cut all rectangles and squares for blocks in half following diagram.

2. Make 48 Block A following diagram. Make 32 Block B following diagram.

3. Stitch Blocks A and B together into 10 rows of 8 blocks each, rotating as shown. Stitch rows together.

4. Piece backing vertically to same size as

batting. Layer and quilt as desired. Trim backing and batting even with top.

5. Stitch binding strips end to end. Press in half lengthwise, wrong sides together. Bind quilt using ⅜″ seam allowance.

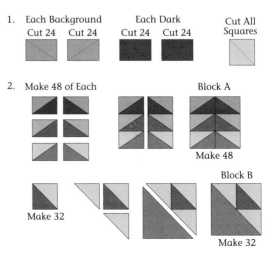

1. Each Background   Each Dark   Cut All Squares
Cut 24   Cut 24   Cut 24   Cut 24

2. Make 48 of Each   Block A
Make 48

Block B
Make 32

Make 32

3.

Appliqued Clothing

Photo on page 29

Materials

purchased apron, denim shirt, or sweatshirt
fabric scraps for applique
fusible web

Directions

Choose applique patterns from other projects in *Home for the Harvest*. We made a 200% enlargement of the pattern on the right side of page 101 for the apron and the denim shirt. If you don't have access to a copier, use patterns at the size given. We used the pattern on page 102 as given (100%) for the sweatshirt. Below are other suggestions for clothing and household use. Enlarge or reduce to the desired size.

Try our patterns on other projects like these! Enlarge or reduce as necessary.

Falling Leaves

Photo on page 25

Approximate size 56x56″

14″ blocks set 4x4

Use 42-44″-wide fabric. When strips appear in the cutting list, cut crossgrain strips (selvage to selvage).

Note: The directions for this quilt require the use of the Pineapple Rule, available by mail from Possibilities®. See page 104.

Yardage

Cream tone-on-tone prints to total	3⅝ yds.
Green prints to total	3¼ yds.
Applique fabrics	scraps up to 6x8″
Backing	3¾ yds.
Binding	⅝ yd.
Batting	62x62″

Cutting Patterns on pages 42-44

Background	8 squares – 3″
	40 strips 2″ wide
	8 strips – 4½″ wide
Green prints	8 squares – 3″
	33 strips 2″ wide
	8 strips – 4½″ wide
Appliques	6 Leaf A
	4 Leaf B
	10 Leaf C
	6 Leaf D
	10 Leaf E
	12 acorns
Binding	6 strips 2½″ wide

Directions

Use ¼″ seam allowance unless otherwise noted.

1. Make 4 each of Blocks A and B and 8 of Block C following directions and diagrams on pages 13 and 14 and using color as shown in block diagrams at right.

2. Lay out blocks, rotating as shown in whole-quilt diagram at right. Blocks A go in the center, Blocks B in the corners, and Blocks C on the sides. Stitch blocks together in horizontal rows.

3. Stitch rows together. Press.

4. Applique quilt using your favorite method. Our favorite method is fusible web, and our patterns are set up for it—reversed for tracing and no seam allowances added. Refer to whole-quilt diagram above for layout.

5. Piece backing to same size as batting. Layer and quilt as desired. Trim backing and batting even with top.

6. Stitch binding strips end to end. Press in half lengthwise, wrong sides together. Bind quilt using ⅜″ seam allowance.

1.

Block A	Block B	Block C
Make 4	Make 4	Make 8

Directions for One Block

Round 1: Mark diagonal lines from corner to corner across wrong side of center square. Cut four 3″ segments from the 2″ strips cut for logs (use four different fabrics). Stitch to opposite sides of center square. Stitch others to remaining sides. Carefully press seam allowances toward outside of block; do not stretch square out of shape.

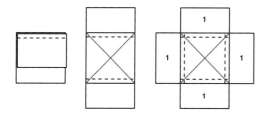

Lay Pineapple Rule on wrong side of block, **inside diagonal lines on ruler on top of seamline and center vertical line matching marked center line on center square.** A horizontal line on ruler may not fall exactly on the horizontal pencil line but should be parallel and equidistant from it. Trim off the two triangles of fabric at corner. Repeat at other corners of block.

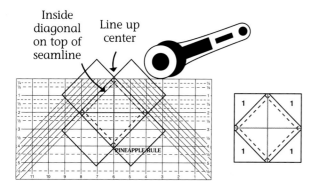

Round 2: Cut four 4½″ segments (different fabrics) and stitch to block as in Round 1. They will be slightly longer than necessary. Press seam allowances to outside of block. Draw lines from corner to corner, keeping right angle at center. Lay ruler on block as before, **lining up the inside diagonal lines on the seamline.** Trim corners.

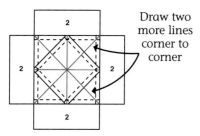

Draw two more lines corner to corner

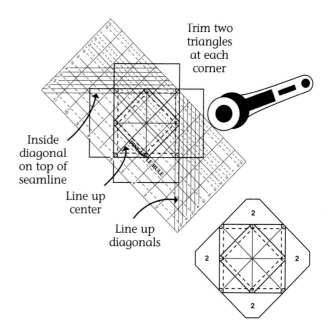

Trim two triangles at each corner

Inside diagonal on top of seamline

Line up center

Line up diagonals

Round 3: Cut four 5″ segments (different fabrics) and stitch to block. Press, being careful not to stretch the block. Trim the corners, **this time lining up the edge of the ruler with the edge of Round 2.** Continue to use center, horizontal, and diagonal guidelines on ruler.

HINT
Try to use the same horizontal guide for each side of every block.

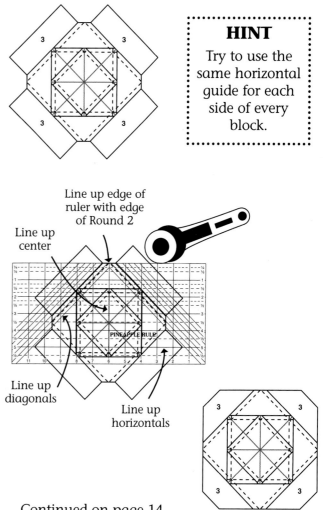

Line up edge of ruler with edge of Round 2

Line up center

Line up diagonals

Line up horizontals

Continued on page 14.

13

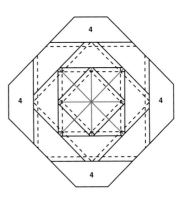

Cut here

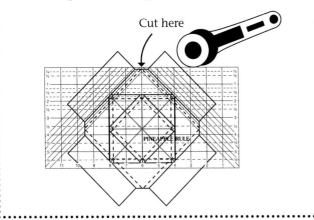

Rounds 5-7: Cut segments (see below) and continue in the same manner as for Round 4.

Round 5 — four 6¼″ segments

Round 6 — four 7″ segments

Round 7 — four 7½″ segments

Round 8 (corner): Cut four 8½″ segments from the 4½″ wide strips in the cutting chart. Stitch to corners of block (corners of block attach to Round 6, center square of block sits square). Press. Line up one corner of the Pineapple Rule with two adjacent sides of the block. Trim both sides of the corner without moving the ruler.

Round 4: Cut four 5½″ segments and stitch to block. Press, being careful not to stretch the block. Trim the corners, **lining up the edge of the ruler with the edge of Round 3.**

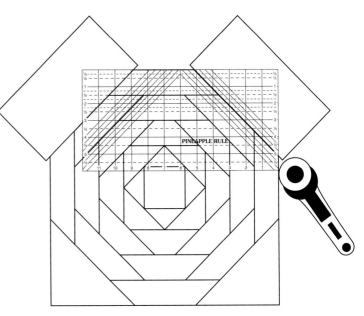

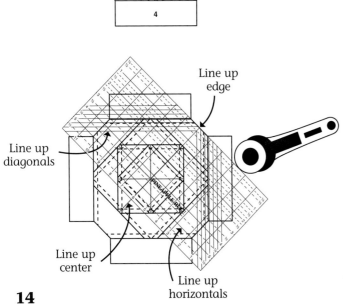

Line up edge

Line up diagonals

Line up center

Line up horizontals

Pumpkins

Photos on pages 21, 52, 53, 64

Approximate height ranges from 6″ to 2½″.

Materials   Makes 1

Main fabric	⅝ yd. (x-large)
	½ yd. (large)
	⅜ yd. (medium)
	¼ yd. (small)
Leaf fabric	1 rectangle – 6x10″ (all sizes)
Base	4″ square felt (all sizes)
Fiberfill	1 lb. for x-large, others less
Fusible web	1 rectangle – 6x10″ (all sizes)
Florist's wire	12-18″ – green or brown
Jute (stem)	3-6″ for small & medium sizes
	36″ for large & x-large sizes
	(can use twig for small &
	medium sizes instead of jute)

Cutting   Patterns on page 39

Main fabric	12 pumpkin segments
Base fabric	1 star-shaped base
Leaf fabric	See Step 4

Directions

Use ¼″ seam allowance unless otherwise noted.

1. Pin and stitch 2 pumpkin segments right sides together on inner curve between dots to make one section. Repeat for other 5 sections. Clip curves.

Two segments make one section

2. Pin right sides of 2 sections together along one outer curve. Stitch between dots. Add a third pumpkin section and stitch between dots on outside curve. Clip curve. Repeat. There will be 2 units of 3 sections (6 segments)

Two Sections

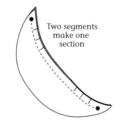

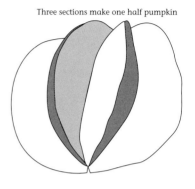

Three sections make one half pumpkin

each. Lay the 2 halves right sides together and stitch each side between dots, leaving an opening on one side for turning.

3. Stuff pumpkin. Whipstitch opening closed.

4. Leaf: Trace 2 leaves on paper side of fusible web. Fuse to wrong side of leaf fabric following manufacturer's directions. Cut out. Remove paper. Lay one leaf right side down on ironing board. Place florist's wire down center of leaf. Lay remaining leaf on top, right side up, and fuse the two leaves together. Twist exposed end of wire around a pencil to form tendril. Bend leaf into desired shape.

5. Stem: For small pumpkin, glue a piece of jute or a twig into hole in top of pumpkin. For medium pumpkin, use 2 pieces of jute or a twig. For large and extra-large pumpkins, make a 4-strand braid: Cross center of two 18″ pieces of jute as shown. Wrap left strand over, under, and over the other three strands. Wrapping tightly will make stem curve. Repeat same motion until stem is desired length. Glue ends together, then glue stem into hole on top of pumpkin.

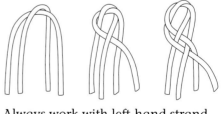

Always work with left-hand strand.
Always go over, under, over.
Tighten at top.

6. Glue pumpkin base over hole on bottom of pumpkin. Glue leaf next to stem.

15

Black Magic

Photo on page 53

Approximate size 66x78″

6″ blocks set with 6″ sashing

Use 42-44″-wide fabric. When strips appear in the cutting list, cut crossgrain strips (selvage to selvage).

Yardage
Background   3½ yds.
Dark prints   ⅛ yd. each of 30 fabrics
Backing   5 yds.
Batting   72x84″

Cutting
Background   18 strips 6½″ wide
Dark prints   1 strip 2½″ wide of each for blocks & binding

Directions

Use ¼″ seam allowance unless otherwise noted.

1. Cut three 6½″ segments from each dark print strip, leaving remainder of each strip uncut for making binding in Step 7. Make 30 blocks following diagram, combining colors as desired.

2. Cut 4 of the background strips into 6½″ segments (twenty-four 6½″ squares needed).

3. Stitch horizontal rows of blocks and background squares together as shown.

4. Stitch alternate rows of blocks and 6½″ background strips together as shown, piecing background strips together as necessary, and starting and ending with rows of blocks.

5. Measure length of quilt. Piece border strips to the measured length and stitch to sides of quilt. Repeat at top and bottom. Press.

6. Piece backing vertically to same size as batting. Layer and quilt as desired. Trim backing and batting even with top.

7. Cut 160 segments 3″ wide from remaining dark print strips. Stitch together to make a binding strip 3″ wide. See diagram. Press seams open. Press strip in half lengthwise, wrong sides together. Bind quilt using ½″ seam allowance.

1.
For 1 Block

7.
Pieced Binding
3″
2″

3-4.

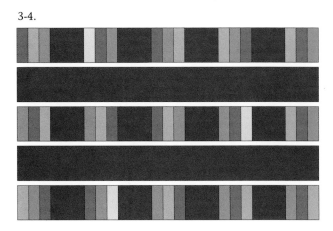

Little Witch **17**

See Photo Index on Page 3

Schoolhouse Plaid

Photo on page 21

Approximate size 65x65″

12″ blocks set with 6″ sashing

Use 42-44″-wide fabric. When strips appear in the cutting list, cut crossgrain strips (selvage to selvage).

Yardage

Background, sashing, borders	3⅓ yds.
Houses & pieced border	⅜ yd. each of 9
Appliques – apples	¼ yd.
leaves & stems	⅛ yd. each
letters	¼ yd.
Backing	4¼ yds.
Binding	⅝ yd.
Batting	71x71″

Cutting   Patterns on pages 46-47, 86

Background	9 A, 9 Ar, 9 C
	9 rectangles 2¾x5½″ – F
	9 rectangles 1¼x7½″ – K
	9 rectangles 1¼x6¾″ – J
	9 rectangles 2x5½″ – I
	6 rect. 6½x12½″ – sashing
	3 strips 6½″ wide – sashing
	6 strips 2¾″ wide – Border 1
	7 strips 4½″ wide – Border 3
Each house fabric	1 B, 1 D
	2 rectangles 1½x2¾″ – E
	1 rectangle 2½x5½″ – G
	2 rectangles 2¼x5½″ – H
	1 square 6¾x6¾″ – L
	10 squares – 3″ – Border 2
Appliques	use photo & whole-quilt diagrams as guides
Binding	7 strips 2½″ wide

Directions

Use ¼″ seam allowance unless otherwise noted.

1. Make 9 house blocks as shown.

2. Stitch 3 rows of blocks and 6½x12½″ sashing rectangles together as shown. Press.

3. Measure width of row. Stitch 6½″ strips to this measurement and stitch to rows of blocks, alternating as shown. Press.

Saying by Henry Ward Beecher

4. Border 1: Measure length of quilt. Piece 2¾″ strips to this measurement and stitch to sides of quilt. Press. Repeat at top and bottom. Press.

5. Border 2: Piece 3″ squares into 2 rows of 21 and 2 rows of 23 squares. Stitch rows of 21 to sides of quilt, adjusting seams as needed. Stitch rows of 23 squares to top and bottom, adjusting as needed.

6. Border 3: Repeat Step 4 with 4½″ strips.

7. Applique quilt using your favorite method. Our favorite method is fusible web, and our patterns are set up for it—reversed for tracing and no seam allowances added. Use our complete alphabet to applique your own favorite saying, if desired.

8. Piece backing to same size as batting. Layer and quilt as desired. Trim backing and batting even with top.

9. Stitch binding strips end to end. Press in half lengthwise, wrong sides together. Bind quilt using ⅜″ seam allowance.

1.

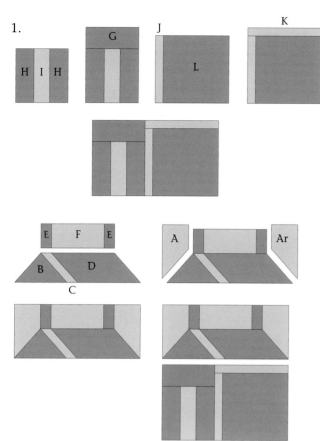

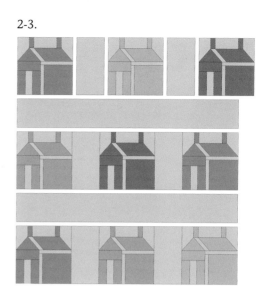

Turkey Stroganoff

1 lb ground turkey
2 tbsp shortening
1 tsp salt
½ tsp pepper
3 tbsp flour
1 small onion, chopped
½ cup cooked mushrooms & juice

1 clove garlic, minced
½-1 cup canned chicken broth
1½ tsp Worcestershire sauce
¼ tsp marjoram
½ cup sour cream

Brown turkey in shortening with salt and pepper. Stir in flour. Add onions, mushrooms, and garlic. Simmer 5 minutes. Add broth, Worcestershire, and marjoram. Simmer 20 minutes, covered. Stir in sour cream. Do not boil. Serve over noodles or rice.

19

THE MOTHER'S HEART

IS THE CHILD'S SCHOOLROOM

Schoolhouse Plaid, Harvest Scarecrow, Pumpkins, A Peck of Apples **21**

See Photo Index on Page 3

Happy Halloween I Spy

Photo on page 28

Approximate size 48 x 60″

Row height approximately 3″

Use 42-44″-wide fabric. When strips appear in the cutting list, cut crossgrain strips (selvage to selvage).

Yardage

Hexagons	5″ square scraps of Halloween prints (157 needed)
Triangles	1⅝ yds.
Border 1	⅝ yd.
Border 2	1⅛ yds.
Backing	3¼ yds.
Binding	⅝ yd.
Batting	54 x 66″

Cutting Patterns on pages 44, 46

Hexagons	157
Triangles	316
Border 1	5 strips 3″ wide
Border 2	6 strips 5½″ wide
Binding	6 strips 2½″ wide

Directions

Use ¼″ seam allowance unless otherwise noted.

1. Make 8 odd rows and 7 even rows referring to diagram. Odd rows have 10 hexagons and begin and end with triangles. Even rows have 11 hexagons and begin and end with hexagons. Press all seams in odd rows to the right and all seams in even rows to the left.

2. Stitch rows together. Press well.

3. Trim sides to straighten edges. Press.

4. Border 1: Measure length of quilt. Piece border strips to the measured length and stitch to sides of quilt. Repeat at top and bottom. Press.

5. Border 2: Repeat Step 4.

6. Optional: Use permanent marking pen to write sayings in Border 1 that describe Halloween prints—A Dozen Black Cats, A Witch Flying an Airplane, and so on. Applique Happy Halloween, I Spy, and candy corn between sayings using patterns on pages 44 and 46.

1.   Odd Rows

Even Rows

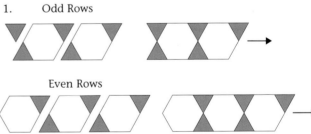

3.   Trim

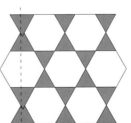

7. Piece backing horizontally to same size as batting. Layer and quilt as desired. Trim backing and batting even with top.

8. Stitch binding strips end to end. Press in half lengthwise, wrong sides together. Bind quilt using ⅜″ seam allowance.

Tie Pillow

Photo on page 60

Makes one 13-14″ pillow

Materials

Blue, red   ½ yd. each
Pillow form   14″

Cutting   Pattern on page 99

One 13½″ square from each fabric
Two from each fabric using pattern piece

Directions

1. Place two tie pieces, one blue and one red, right sides together. Stitch around curved edge with a ¼″ seam allowance, leaving 13½″ straight side open for turning. Turn and press. Repeat with other tie pieces.

2. Lay red square right side up on table. Lay one tie piece on square, raw edges even, with red side down. Pin. Fold up tie end and pin to center of square. Repeat with other tie piece on opposite side of square. Stitch each tie piece to square using ¼″ seam allowance.

3. Lay blue square right sides together on red square. Pin all raw edges.

4. Stitch around three sides of square, leaving one side with tie piece open for turning. Trim corners, turn, and press.

5. Insert pillow form into cover. Hand stitch opening closed.

6. Tie ends on one side or the other.

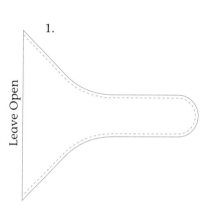

1.

4.

23

24 Indian Summer, Harvest Scarecrow
See Photo Index on Page 3

Forest Floor, Falling Leaves **25**
See Photo Index on Page 3

Forest Floor

Photos on pages 25, 32

Approximate size 66x81″

3″ squares set 16x21

6″ applique border & 3″ pieced border

Use 42-44″-wide fabric. When strips appear in the cutting list, cut crossgrain strips (selvage to selvage).

Yardage

Squares & flowers	⅜ yd. each of 20 fabrics
Vine	¼ yd.
Applique border	1½ yds.
Backing	5⅛ yds.
Binding	¾ yd.
Batting	72x87″
Fusible web	3¼ yds.

Cutting   Patterns on page 45

Squares	430 squares – 3½″
Appliques	see Step 5a of directions
Applique border	7 strips 6½″ wide
Binding	8 strips 2½″ wide

Directions

Use ¼″ seam allowance unless otherwise noted.

1. Stitch squares together into 21 rows of 16.

2. Stitch rows together. Press well.

3. Measure length of quilt. Piece applique border strips to the measured length and stitch to sides of quilt. Repeat at top and bottom. Press.

4. Stitch squares into 2 rows of 25 and 2 rows of 22. Stitch rows of 25 to sides of quilt, adjusting seams as needed to make them fit. Stitch rows of 22 to top and bottom, adjusting as needed. Press.

5. Applique: Our favorite method is fusible web, and this quilt uses an easy fusible web vine technique. Patterns have no seam allowances added.

   a. Trace appliques to fusible web: 8 each Flowers A & B, 12 Flower C, 60 D, 84 E, 28 vine segments, 4 vine corner segments, and 4 vine corner segments reversed.

   b. Fuse to desired fabrics and cut out.

   c. Fuse vine segments to one corner quadrant of border as shown in diagram. Repeat for other four corners of quilt.

   d. Fuse flowers and leaves to one corner quadrant of quilt along vine as shown, making sure to cover joins in vine. Repeat for other four corners of quilt. Stitch in place with machine zigzag or buttonhole stitch.

6. Piece backing vertically to same size as batting. Layer and quilt as desired. Trim backing and batting even with top.

7. Stitch binding strips end to end. Press in half lengthwise, wrong sides together. Bind quilt using ⅜″ seam allowance.

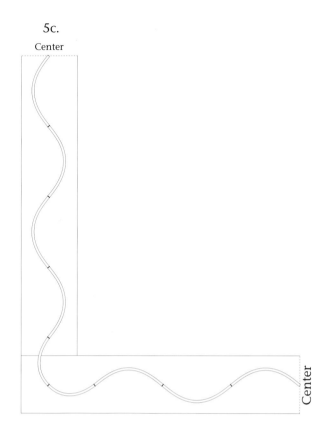

5c.

Center

Center

5d.

Plate Charmers

Photos on pages 49, 52, 64. Sizes vary.

Materials Makes 1

2 round clear glass plates for each place setting
2 squares background fabric larger than plates
fabric scraps for applique
fusible web
paper for making pattern

Directions

1. Make a round pattern of the full size of the plate or just the size of the base at the center.

2. Choose applique patterns from other projects in *Home for the Harvest*. We enlarged the candy corn on a photocopier for the spider example below, but all other patterns were used in the sizes given.

3. Prepare fusible web applique pieces. Center design on a square of fabric 2-3″ bigger than the circular pattern. Fuse in place.

4. Backing: Bond a square of fusible web to wrong side of Plate Charmer. Peel paper and fuse to wrong side of the other square.

5. Using paper pattern, cut out Plate Charmer.

6. Place Plate Charmer between two plates.

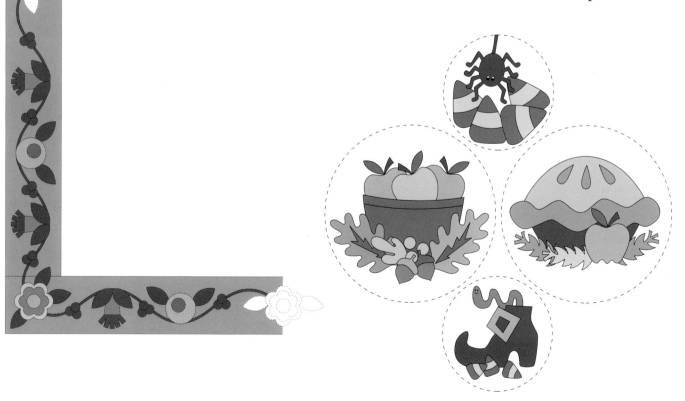

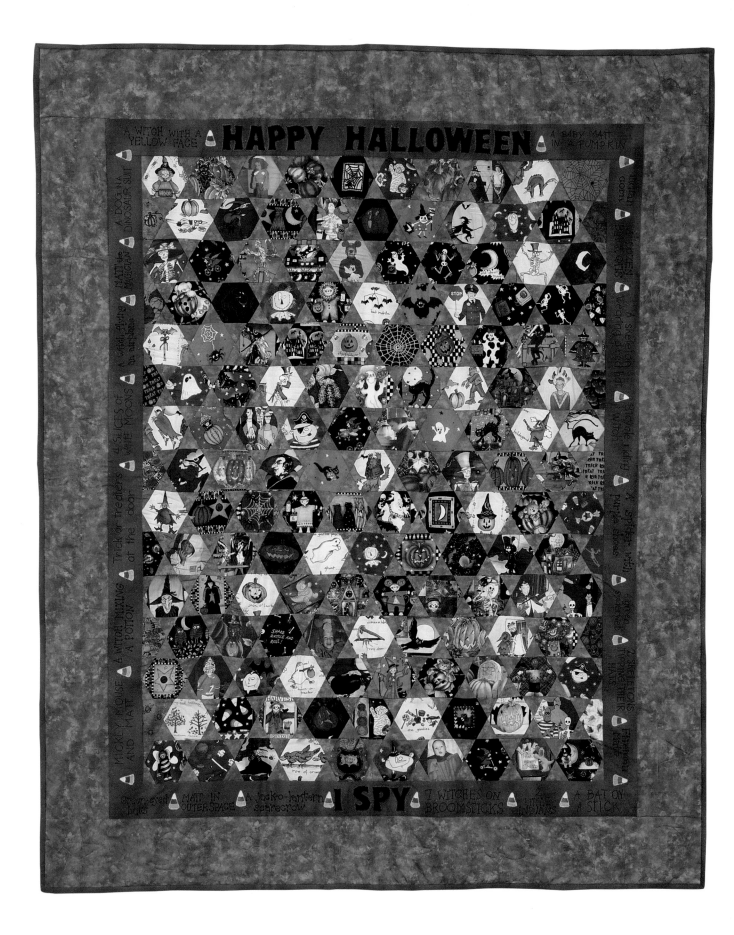

Included are Halloween photos of Ann Petersen's son, Matt.

Sunrise Sunset

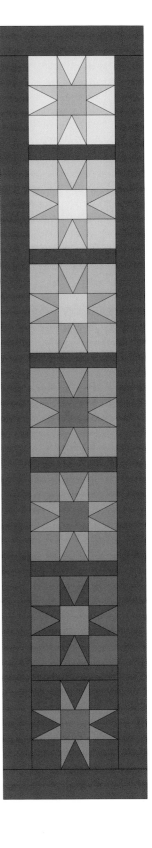

Photo on back cover

Approximate size 10x52″

6″ blocks set with 1″ sashing & 2″ border

Use 42-44″-wide fabric. When strips appear in the cutting list, cut crossgrain strips (selvage to selvage).

Yardage

Blocks	⅛ yd. each of 21 mottled solids or tone-on-tones – 3 yellows, 3 yellow oranges, 3 oranges, 3 red oranges, 3 reds, 3 red violets, 3 violets
Sashing/border	½ yd.
Backing	1 yd.
Binding	⅓ yd.
Batting	14 x 56″

Cutting   Pattern on page 80

Blocks	Use 3 fabrics for each block as listed in yardage chart (i.e., 3 yellows in one block, 3 yellow oranges in one block, etc.). Side units are paper-pieced. 1 center & 4 corner squares – 2½″
Sashing	6 rectangles – 1½ x 6½″
Border	3 strips 2½″ wide
Binding	4 strips 2½″ wide

Directions

Use ¼″ seam allowance unless otherwise noted.

1. Make 7 blocks using paper piecing pattern on page 80, Step 2 of directions on page 50, and Step 2 diagrams on page 51. Press.

2. Stitch blocks together in order from lightest to darkest with sashing rectangles between them. Press.

3. Measure length of quilt. Piece border strips to the measured length and stitch to sides of quilt. Repeat at top and bottom. Press.

4. Piece backing horizontally to same size as batting. Layer and quilt as desired. Trim backing and batting even with top.

5. Stitch binding strips end to end. Press in half lengthwise, wrong sides together. Bind quilt using ⅜″ seam allowance.

Cookie Caddy

Photo on page 64.   For 8″ square glass dish.

Materials

Prewash fabric and batting so caddy will fit after laundering.

Fabric for outside – purple	½ yd.
Fabric for inside – orange	⅝ yd.
Applique fabric – black	⅛ yd.
Batting – thin cotton	15″ square
Heavy cardboard	

Cutting   Bat pattern for sides on page 36

Outside	1 square – 15″
Inside	1 square – 14″
Center pocket	1 rectangle – 9x9½″
Side pockets	4 rectangles – 6x9″
Ties	8 rectangles – 1½x12″
Applique	4 bats
Cardboard	1 square – 7¼″
	4 rectangles – 2x7¼″

Directions

1. Layer in order and pin well:
   a. batting square
   b. outside fabric square, right side up
   c. inside fabric square, right side down, centered on others

2. Stitch around small square with a ⅜″ seam allowance, leaving 4″ open on one side for turning. Trim large squares even with small square. Clip corners. Turn through opening so batting is sandwiched between fabric layers. Press. Pin opening closed. Topstitch very close to entire outside edge of caddy.

3. Lightly mark a diagonal 2″ grid on outside of caddy and machine quilt on the lines.

4. Mark fold lines on inside of caddy, as shown, 2½″ from each side.

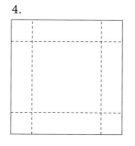

4.

5. Applique bats on each side panel on outside of caddy, centered from side to side, tops of heads about ½″ from outside edge.

6. Hem one 9″ side of center pocket piece: Press ½″ to wrong side then press ½″ to wrong side again. Stitch close to fold. Pocket should measure 8½″ high by 9″ wide.

7. Lay pocket wrong side down on inside of caddy, matching hemmed edge with one marked fold line. See diagram. Tuck under and pin the three raw edges to meet marked fold lines on caddy. Press pocket. Stitch pinned edges very close to folds.

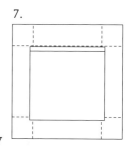

7.

8. Press the 1½x12″ pieces for ties in half lengthwise, wrong sides together. Unfold. Press long raw edges in to meet pressed line. Fold in one end, then refold along center line. Stitch across end and along double-folded edge.

9. Press the four 6x9″ pieces for the side pockets in half lengthwise, wrong sides together, to 3x9″. Lay one side pocket on side of caddy with fold next to edge of center pocket. See diagram. Tuck under and pin the three raw edges to meet marked fold lines an outside edge of caddy. Press pocket. Repeat for other three side pockets.

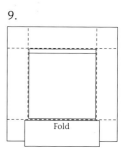

9.

Fold

10. Tuck raw end of a tie under corner of side pocket at each corner of caddy as shown. Pin in place. Stitch pinned edges of pockets, catching ties in stitching.

11. Trim cardboard pieces slightly, if necessary, to fit pockets. Slide into pockets. Fold sides of caddy up and tie each corner in a bow.

10.

Stencilled Pillows

Photo on page 53

We used Red Oak and Sugar Maple stencils by Country Stencils, 9510 Daybreak Dr., Knoxville, TN 37931. Phone and fax 423-769-3887. For the paint, we used acid free pigment inkpads that were labeled for heat-setting on fabric.

Wreath Pillow 16″ square

Materials

Background – tan	½ yd.
Backing & Border 2	⅝ yd.
Border 1	⅙ yd.
Stuffing	1 lb.

Cutting

Background	14″ square
Backing	18″ square
Border 2	four 2½ x 20″ strips
Border 1	four 1½ x 16″ strips

Directions

Use ¼″ seam allowance unless otherwise noted.

1. Using Red Oak stencil, stencil a centered 8″ wreath on background square. Adding an extra single leaf here and there fills out the wreath shape. See photo. Heat press following manufacturer's directions. Trim square down to 10½″, recentering wreath if necessary.

2. Stitch Border 1 strips to opposite sides of background, trimming ends even with background square. Stitch Border 1 strips to remaining sides of block, trimming ends. Press.

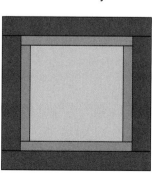

3. Repeat Step 2 with Border 2 strips.

4. Center pillow top on backing square, right sides together. Pin well. Stitch around pillow top, leaving a 4″ opening for turning. Trim away excess backing. Trim corners. Turn right side out.

5. Stuff pillow. Hand stitch opening closed.

Maple Leaf Pillow

10 x 15″ rectangle

Materials

Background – tan	¼ yd.
Backing & Border 2	½ yd.
Border 1	⅛ yd.
Stuffing	½ lb.

Cutting

Background	7 x 12″ rectangle
Backing	12 x 17″ rectangle
Border 2	four 2½ x 16″ strips
Border 1	four 1½ x 12″ strips

Directions

Use ¼″ seam allowance unless otherwise noted.

1. Using Sugar Maple stencil, stencil four double-leaf motifs, centered, on background rectangle. See photo. Heat press following manufacturer's directions. Trim to 4½ x 9½″, recentering if necessary.

2. Stitch Border 1 strips to short sides of background rectangle, trimming ends even with background. Stitch Border 1 strips to remaining sides of rectangle, trimming ends. Press.

3. Repeat Step 2 with Border 2 strips.

4. Center pillow top on backing rectangle, right sides together. Pin well. Stitch around pillow top, leaving a 4″ opening for turning. Trim away excess backing. Trim corners. Turn right side out.

5. Stuff pillow. Hand stitch opening closed.

Patterns are reversed for tracing to fusible web

Little Witch

Permission granted to photocopy for individual use.

NOTE: For large version of Little Witch, page 5, make 140% photocopy. Copy to 11x17" sheets of paper, if possible, or use 8½x11" sheets and tape them together. Always place book on copier in same direction to minimize distortion.

Use permanent marker for eyes

34

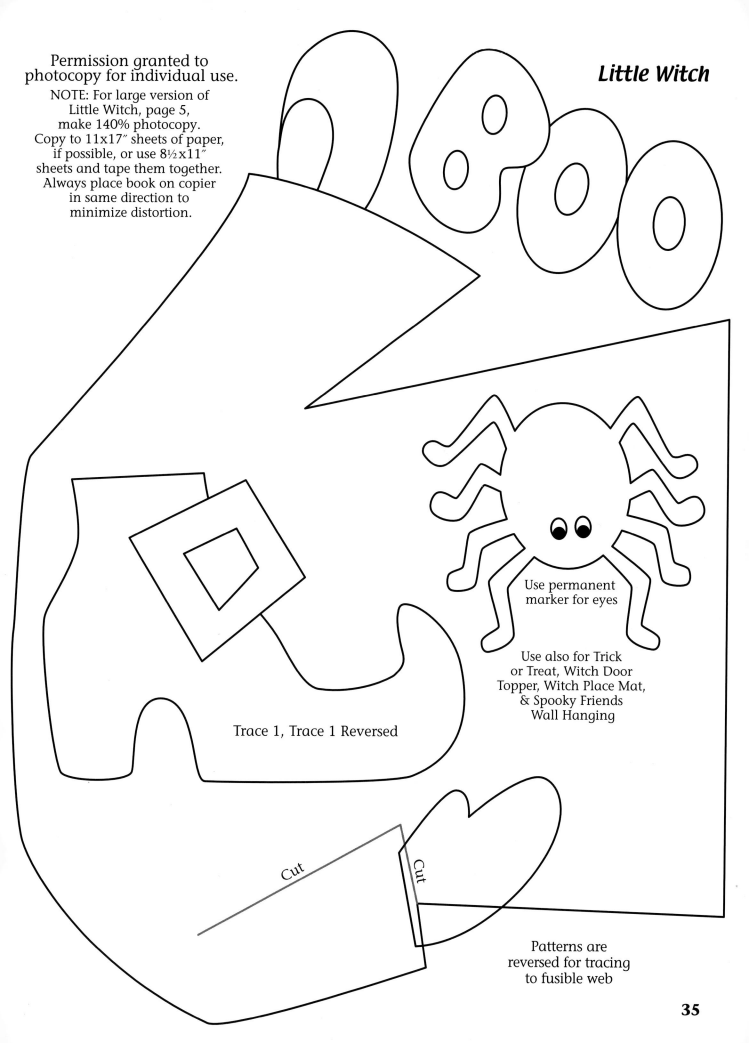

NOTE: For large version of
Little Witch, page 5,
make 140% photocopy.
Copy to 11x17″ sheets of paper,
if possible, or use 8½x11″
sheets and tape them together.
Always place book on copier
in same direction to
minimize distortion.

Little Witch

Use permanent
marker for eyes

Use also for Trick
or Treat, Witch Door
Topper, Witch Place Mat,
& Spooky Friends
Wall Hanging

Trace 1, Trace 1 Reversed

Cut

Cut

Patterns are
reversed for tracing
to fusible web

35

Little Witch

Permission granted to photocopy for individual use.

NOTE: For large version of Little Witch, page 5, make 140% photocopy. Copy to 11x17″ sheets of paper, if possible, or use 8½ x11″ sheets and tape them together. Always place book on copier in same direction to minimize distortion.

Use permanent marker for eyes

Use also for Trick or Treat, Cookie Caddy, Dracula Place Mat, & Spooky Friends Wall Hanging

Use also for
Trick or Treat
(trace 1, trace
1 reversed)

Use permanent
marker for eyes

Little Witch

Witch Place Mat
Spooky Friends
Wall Hanging

Patterns are
reversed for tracing
to fusible web

Match to dotted
line below
for full pattern

Permission granted to
photocopy for individual use.
NOTE: For large version of
Little Witch, page 5,
make 140% photocopy.
Copy to 11x17″ sheets of paper,
if possible, or use 8½x11″
sheets and tape them together.
Always place book on copier
in same direction to
minimize distortion.

Trace 1, Trace 1 Reversed

Little Witch

Use permanent
marker for eyes

HAPPY

O

MEN

Permission granted to
photocopy for individual use.

NOTE: For large version of Little Witch,
page 5, make 140% photocopy.
Copy to 11x17″ sheets of paper,
if possible, or use 8½x11″ sheets
and tape them together. Always
place book on copier in same
direction to minimize distortion.

38

Patterns are
reversed for tracing
to fusible web

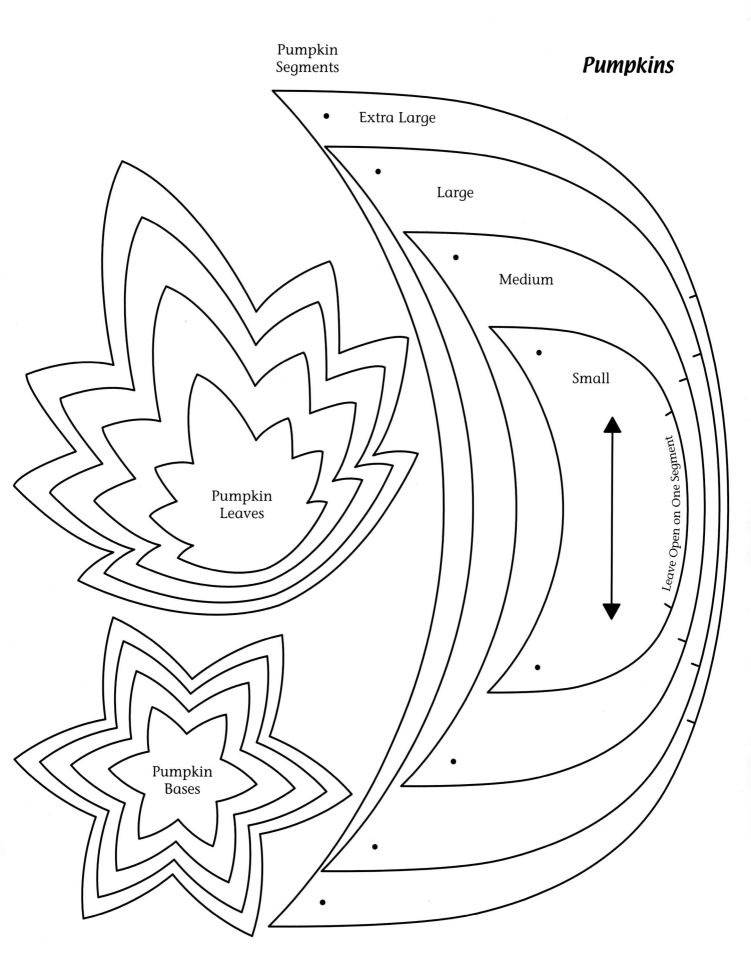

Pumpkin
Segments

Pumpkins

Extra Large

Large

Medium

Small

Leave Open on One Segment

Pumpkin
Leaves

Pumpkin
Bases

39

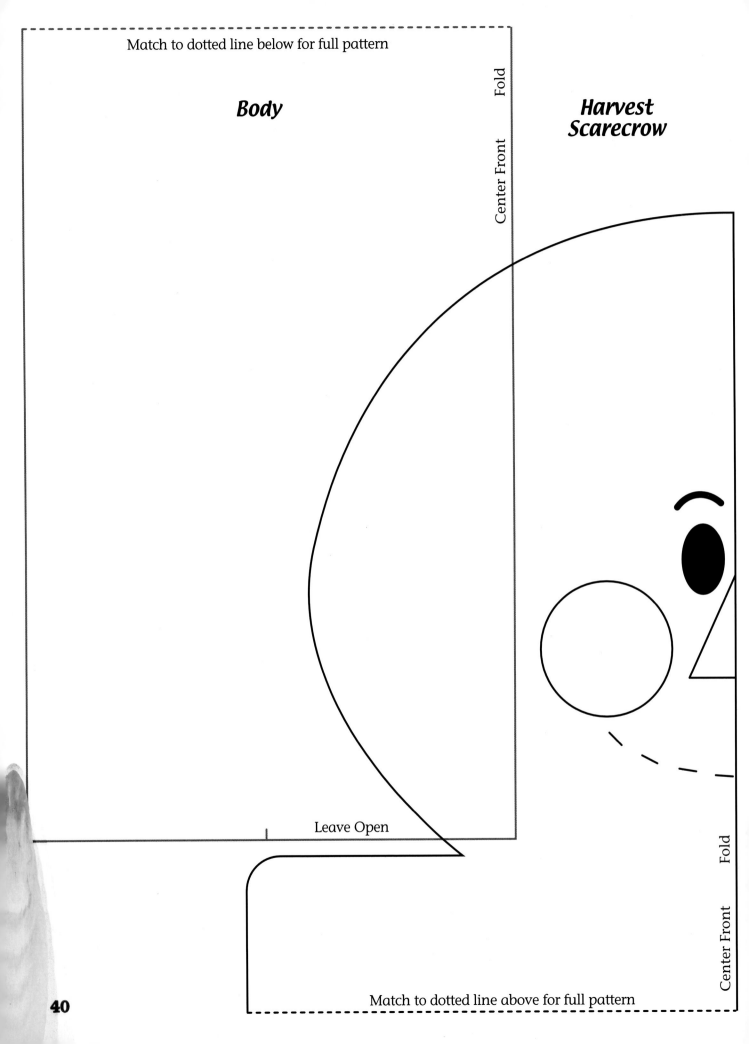

Match to dotted line below for full pattern

Body

Harvest Scarecrow

Fold

Center Front

Leave Open

Fold

Center Front

Match to dotted line above for full pattern

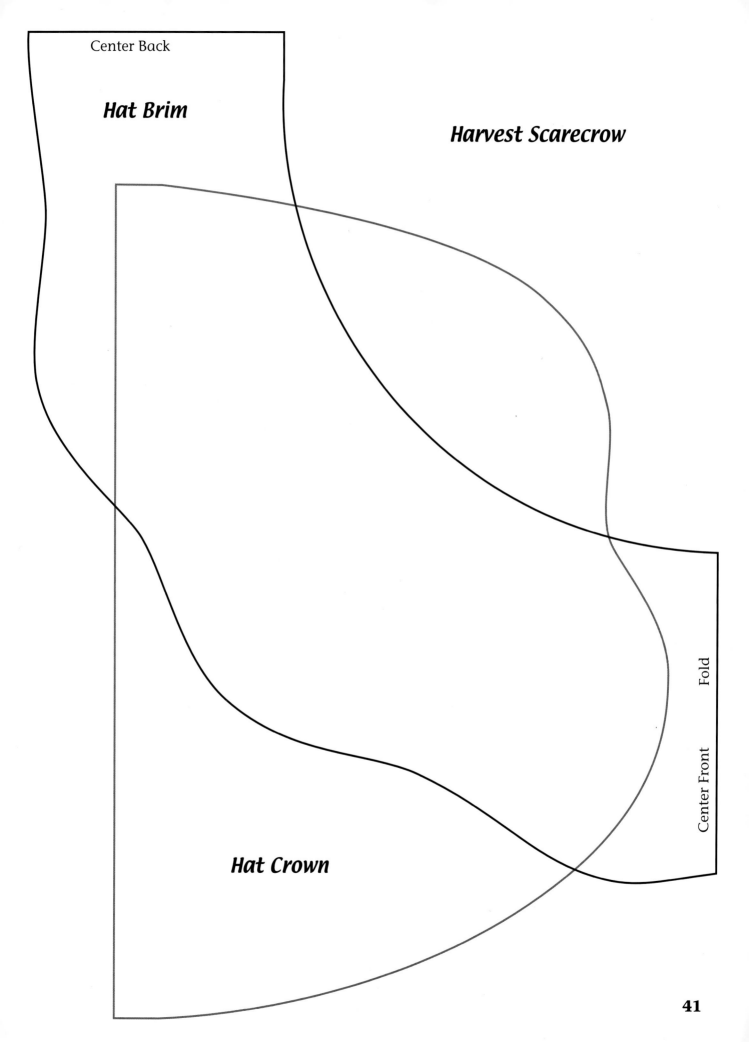

Center Back

Hat Brim

Harvest Scarecrow

Fold

Center Front

Hat Crown

Center Back

41

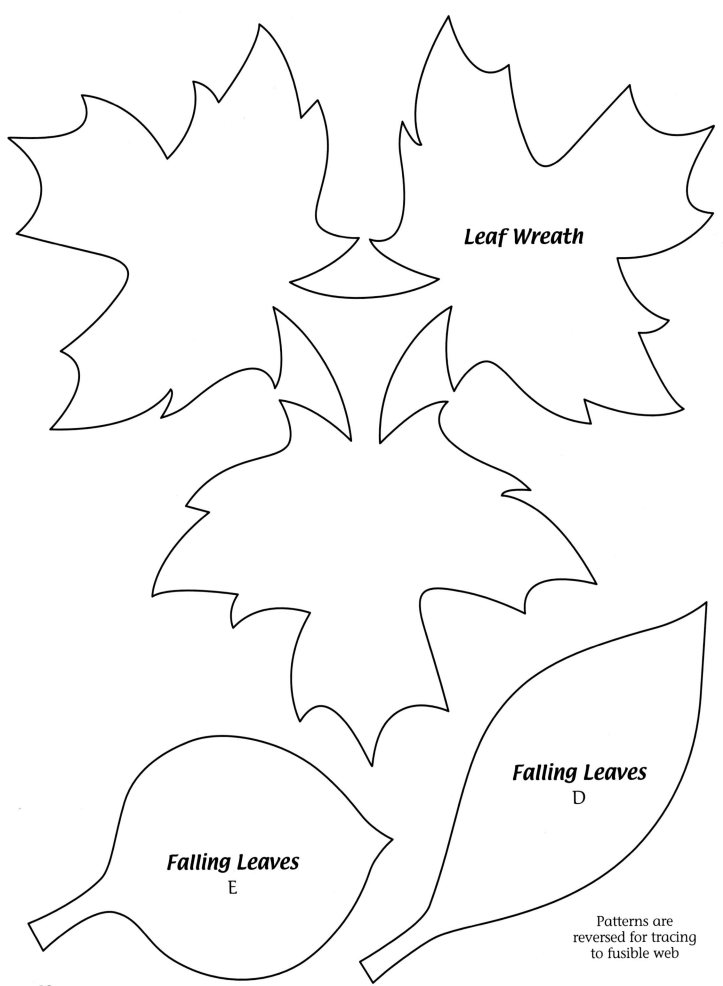

Leaf Wreath

Falling Leaves
D

Falling Leaves
E

Patterns are
reversed for tracing
to fusible web

Patterns are
reversed for tracing
to fusible web

A

Falling Leaves

C

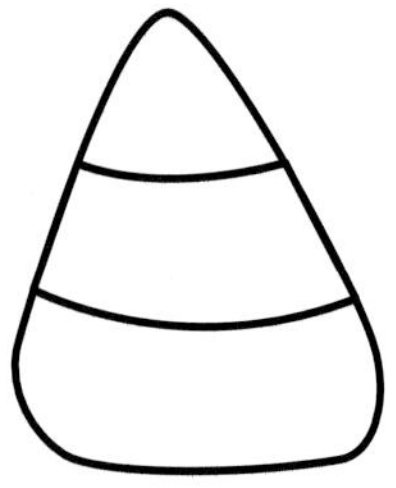

Optional
Border 1
Applique

Happy Halloween I Spy

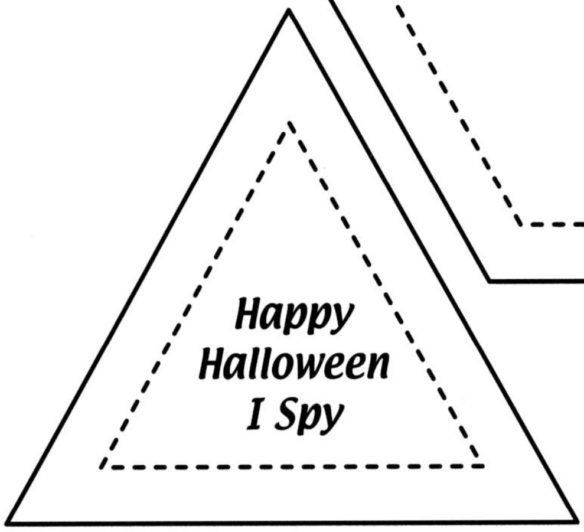

*Happy
Halloween
I Spy*

*Autumn
Table
Runner*

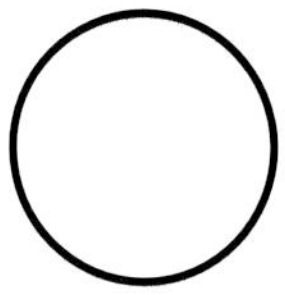

Trace 10, trace
10 reversed

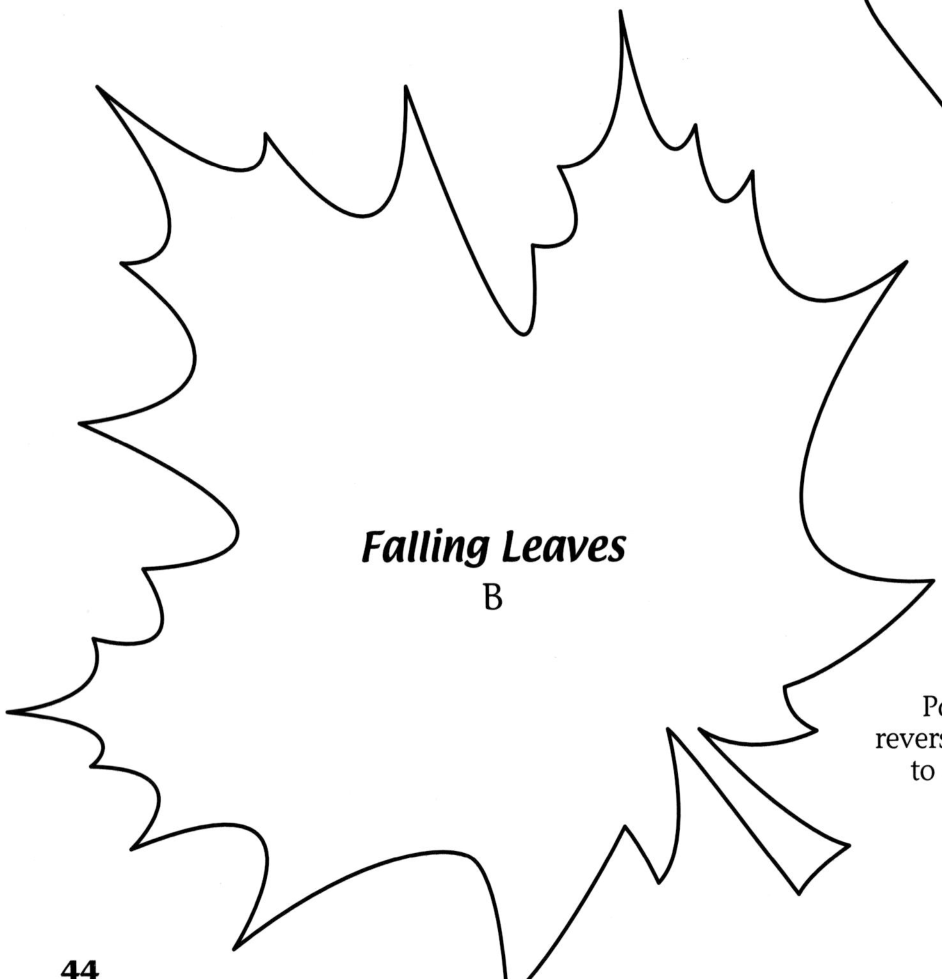

Falling Leaves
B

Patterns are
reversed for tracing
to fusible web

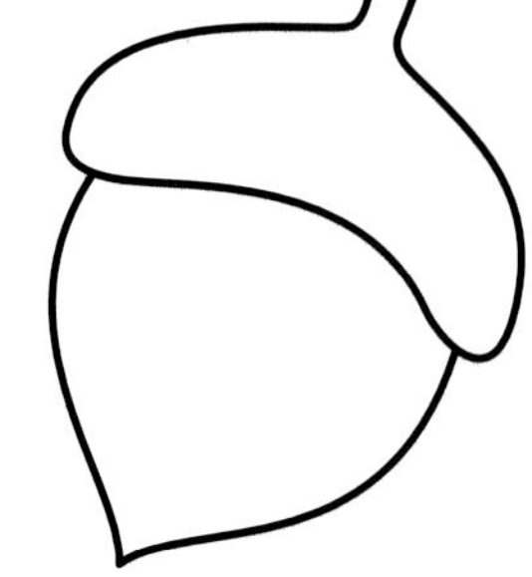

44

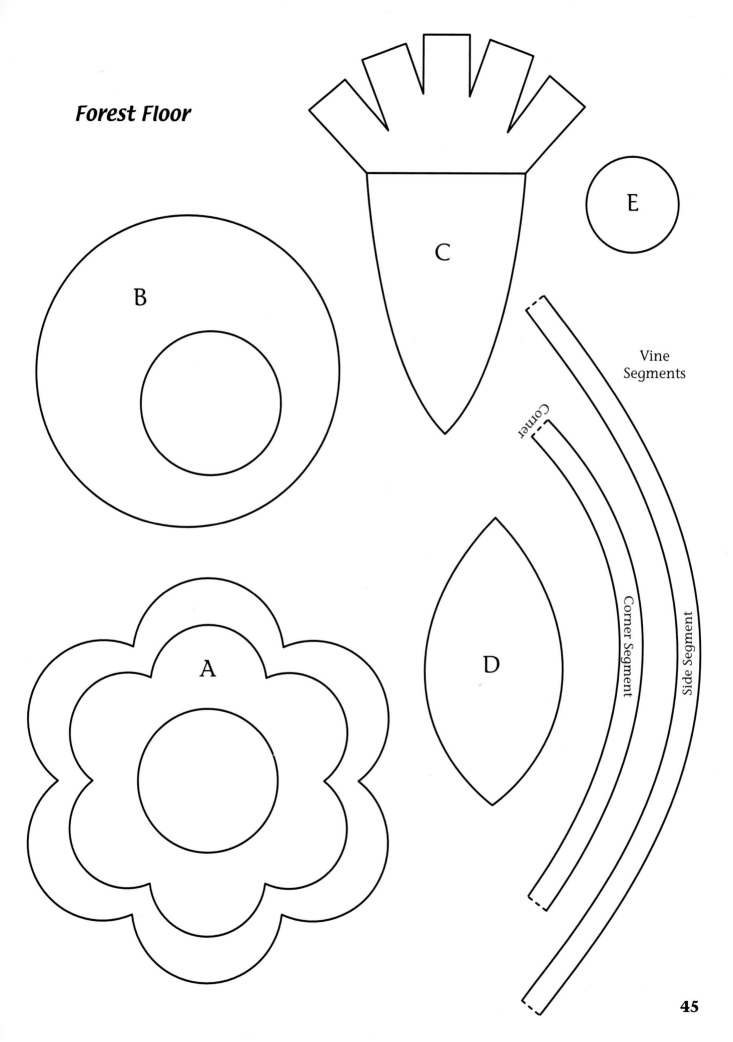

Forest Floor

B

C

E

Vine
Segments

Corner

Corner Segment

Side Segment

A

D

45

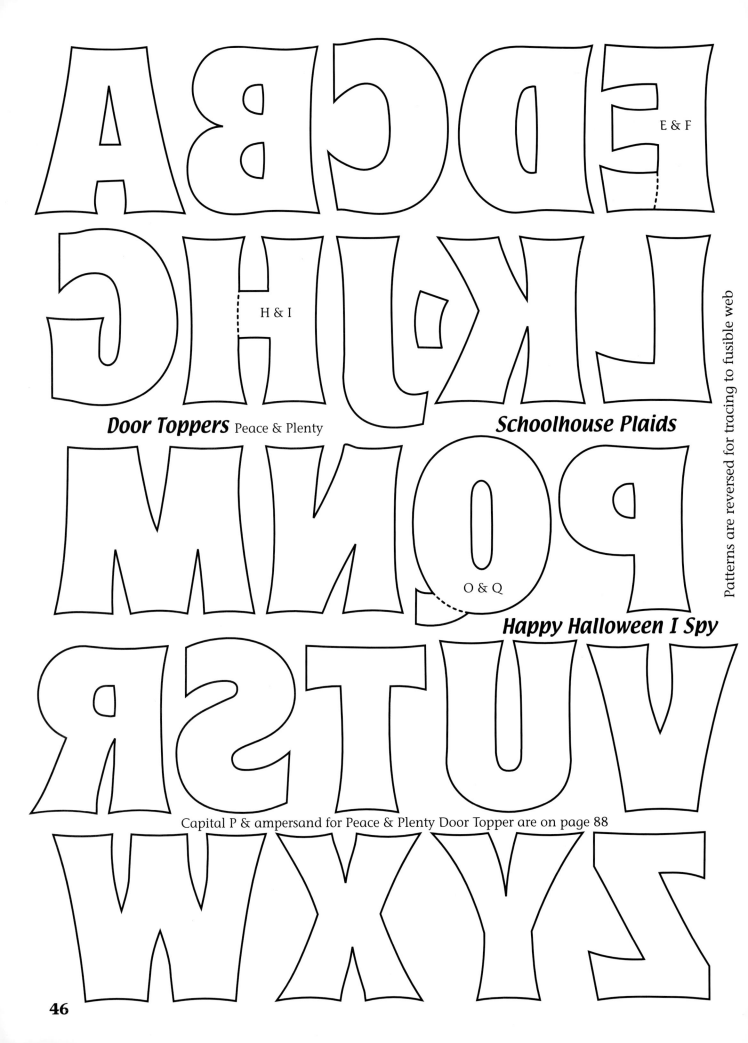

A B C D E

E & F

G H I J K L

H & I

Door Toppers Peace & Plenty

Schoolhouse Plaids

M N O P

Q R S T U V

O & Q

Happy Halloween I Spy

W X Y Z

Patterns are reversed for tracing to fusible web

Capital P & ampersand for Peace & Plenty Door Topper are on page 88

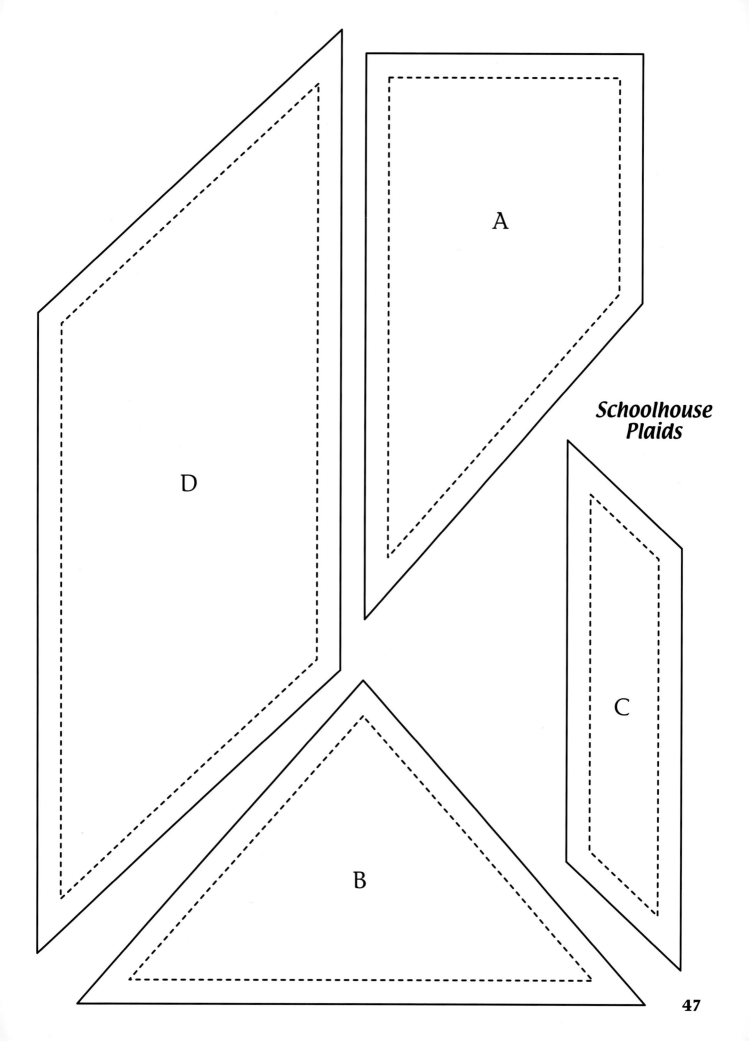

A

*Schoolhouse
Plaids*

D

C

B

47

Harvest Moon & Trick or Treat

Photos of Harvest Moon on pages 52, 53

Photo of Trick or Treat on page 49

Approximate size 28x35″

6″ blocks set 3x4 with 1″ sashing

Use 42-44″-wide fabric. When strips appear in the cutting list, cut crossgrain strips (selvage to selvage).

Yardage

Background	½ yd.
Appliques	branch – 5x14″
	post & cornstalks – 2x20″
	others – scraps up to 10x12″
Sashing	½ yd.
Border	½ yd. OR ⅛ yd. each of 4 fabrics
Backing	1 yd.
Binding	⅜ yd.
Batting	32x39″

Cutting Patterns on pages 35-37, 72-79

Background	12 squares – 6½″
Appliques	Use photo & whole-quilt diagram as guides. Cut one post 1x8″ and two cornstalks ⅝x13½″.
Sashing	16 rectangles – 1½x6½″
	5 pieces – 1½x22½″
Border	4 strips 3½″ wide
Binding	4 strips 2½″ wide

Directions

Follow Steps 4-8 of I Love Apple Pie directions, page 50.

Harvest Moon

Trick or Treat

Trick or Treat, Harvest Scarecrow, Plate Charmers **49**

See Photo Index on Page 3

I Love Apple Pie

Photo on page 32

Approximate size 28x35″

6″ blocks set 3x4 with 1″ sashing

Use 42-44″-wide fabric. When strips appear in the cutting list, cut crossgrain strips (selvage to selvage).

Yardage

Backgrounds	tan scraps – nine-patch blocks
	6½″ squares – pie & basket blocks
	⅛ yd. ea. – star & wrench blocks
Star block	⅛ yd. for points, scrap for center
Wrench block	⅛ yd.
Appliques	tree trunk – 8x20″
	leaves – ⅛ yd.
	others – scraps up to 10x10″
Sashing & border	⅞ yd.
Backing	1 yd.
Binding	⅜ yd.
Batting	32x39″

Cutting Patterns on pages 80-82

Backgrounds	72 squares – 2½″ – nine-patches
	2 squares – 6½″ – pie & basket
Star block	4 squares – 2½″ – corners
	(side units are paper-pieced)
Wrench	2 squares – 2⅞″ – corners
	4 rectangles – 1½x2½″ – sides
	1 square – 2½″ – center
Star block	1 square – 2½″ – center
	(side units are paper-pieced)
Wrench block	2 squares – 2⅞″ – corners
	4 rectangles – 1½x2½″ – sides
Appliques	use photo & whole-quilt diagram as guides
Sashing	16 rectangles – 1½x6½″
	5 pieces – 1½x22½″
Border	4 strips 3½″ wide
Binding	4 strips 2½″ wide

Directions

Use ¼″ seam allowance unless otherwise noted.

1. Stitch 8 nine-patch blocks together as shown.

2. Make 4 photocopies of pattern on page 80 for side unit of star block. Paper piece 4 units. Finish making star block as shown.

3. Cut 2⅞″ squares in half diagonally. Make wrench block as shown.

4. Stitch blocks and sashing pieces together as shown.

5. Border: Measure length of quilt. Cut border strips to the measured length and stitch to sides of quilt. Repeat at top and bottom. Press.

6. Applique quilt using your favorite method. Our favorite method is fusible web, and our patterns are set up for it—reversed for tracing and no seam allowances added.

7. Layer top with backing and batting. Quilt. Trim backing and batting even with top.

8. Stitch binding strips together end to end. Press in half lengthwise, wrong sides together. Bind quilt using ⅜″ seam allowance.

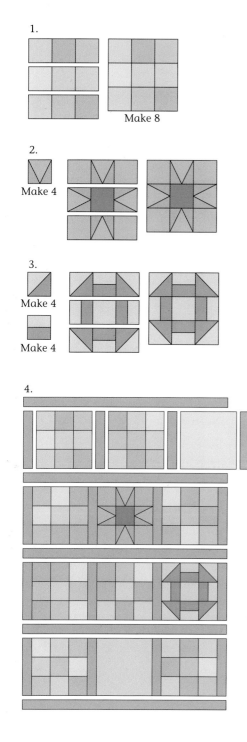

1.

Make 8

2.

Make 4

3.

Make 4

Make 4

4.

A Peck of Apples

Photos on pages 21, 32

Approximate height 4″

Materials Makes 1
Main fabric   8″ square
Leaf fabric   6x4″ rectangle
Fiberfill   small amount
Embroidery floss   brown

Cutting   Patterns on page 86
Main fabric   1 square – 8″
Leaf fabric   2 leaves

Directions

Use ¼″ seam allowance unless otherwise noted.

1. Place 2 leaves right sides together and stitch, leaving bottom edge open. Trim point and turn right side out.

2. For apple, fold 8″ square of fabric in quarters. Place apple pattern piece on fabric, matching folds and cut out.

3. Open apple piece halfway. With right sides together, sew both outer edges.

4. Refold, aligning seams and raw edges. Pleat bottom of leaf and insert into top of apple, raw edges even. Pin. Sew curved seam, leaving open between marks on one side.

5. Turn apple through opening.

6. Stuff softly.

7. Thread long needle with 6 strands of brown floss and tie 2-3 knots at end. Insert needle at center bottom of apple and pull out right next to leaf at top. Pull thread up snugly. Reinsert needle next to where floss exited and pull out at center bottom next to knots. Knot off. Apple should be indented at top and bottom.

8. Finish stuffing apple, filling out the sides.

9. Slipstitch opening closed.

52 Harvest Moon, Pumpkins, Harvest Scarecrow, Autumn Table Runner, Plate Charmers

See Photo Index on Page 3

Black Magic, Harvest Moon, Stencilled Pillows, Pumpkins, Bear Tracks **53**

See Photo Index on Page 3

Pumpkin Patch

This whimsical pumpkin quilt was made by some of our employees. We made a diagram of the quilt and let people choose which size and shape block they wanted to make. Everyone used their own fabrics and their own ideas. For your use, we have included patterns for four of the blocks from our quilt plus one other pattern that wasn't used for our quilt but was too cute to leave out of the book (see pages 100-103). Combining parts of these patterns with others of your own will allow you to make even more blocks. Applique patterns from other projects in the book can be used as well by enlarging or reducing them on a copy machine. See sketches of other blocks from the quilt on page 55.

The best thing about a group quilt is the creative detail that makes each block so unique. Photo transfers add meaningful personal touches. Novelty fabrics and cutouts from preprinted fabrics provide texture and make details possible that would be difficult otherwise.

Be sure to make a chart on muslin for the back of your group quilt that includes the participants' names and the year the quilt was made. See the name chart on page 55 that went on our quilt. It could be written with permanent markers, embroidered, typed, or computer generated. Just cut it out and applique it to the back of the quilt for a permanent record.

Photo on page 56

Approximate size 74x74″

Blocks set with 2″ sashing

Use 42-44″-wide fabric. When strips appear in the cutting list, cut crossgrain strips (selvage to selvage).

Yardage

Background	3¾ yds.
Sashing	1⅝ yds.
Border 1	⅓ yd.
Border 2	1 yd.
Backing	4¾ yds.
Binding	⅔ yd.
Batting	80x80″

Cutting

Backgrounds – measurements are given width by height and include seam allowance

1	12½x6½″	10	8½x18½″	19	8½x18½″
2	8½x6½″	11	6½x6½″	20	6½x6½″
3	22½x8½″	12	6½x10½″	21	6½x10½″
4	20½x16½″	13	8½x6½″	22	16½x8½″
5	8½x18½″	14	8½x6½″	23	16½x12½″
6	6½x8½″	15	18½x16½″	24	8½x8½″
7	8½x8½″	16	8½x14½″	25	6½x8½″
8	8½x8½″	17	14½x14½″	26	6½x8½″
9	6½x8½″	18	24½x8½″	27	8½x8½″

Appliques – some patterns are on pages 100-103

Sashing	20 strips – 2½″ wide
Border 1	7 strips 1¼″ wide
Border 2	8 strips 3¾″ wide
Binding	8 strips 2½″ wide

Directions

Use ¼″ seam allowance unless otherwise noted.

1. Get friends to make the 27 blocks.

2. Stitch blocks together with sashing strips using diagram as a guide for seaming. Press well.

3. Border 1: Measure length of quilt. Piece border strips to the measured length and stitch to sides of quilt. Repeat at top and bottom. Press.

4. Border 2: Repeat Step 3.

5. Piece backing to same size as batting. Layer and quilt as desired. Trim backing and batting even with top.

6. Stitch binding strips together end to end. Press in half lengthwise, wrong sides together. Bind quilt using 3⁄8″ seam allowance.

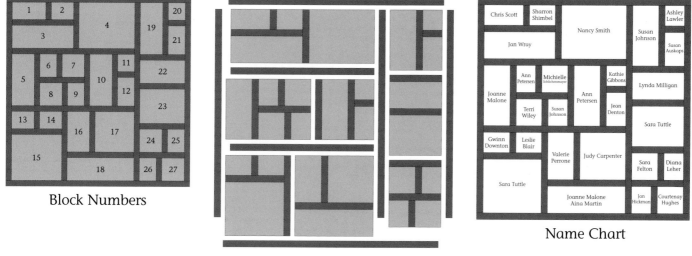

Block Numbers

Piecing Order

Name Chart

Block 18

Block 16

Block 17

Block 22

Not Quite Amish Quilt, Amish Pillow, Harvest Scarecrow, Leaf Wreath **57**
See Photo Index on Page 3

Not Quite Amish Quilt

Photo on page 57

Approximate size 85x85″

Use 42-44″-wide fabric. When strips appear in the cutting list, cut crossgrain strips (selvage to selvage).

Yardage   Solids or mottled solids

Black	2⅜ yds.
Purple	2⅜ yds.
Teal	1¼ yds.
Brick red	1⅜ yds.
Olive	⅝ yd.
Gold	½ yd.
Rust	¼ yd.
Backing	7⅞ yds.
Binding	¾ yd.
Batting	91x91″

Cutting

Nine-patch blocks – 13½″

Black	1 strip – 2″ wide
Purple	4 strips – 2″ wide
Teal	4 strips – 2″ wide
Brick red	1 strip – 2″ wide
Olive	1 strip – 2″ wide
Gold	1 strip – 2″ wide
Black	5 squares – 14″ 4 strips – 7½″ wide
Purple	2 squares – 33¾″
Teal	8 strips – 3½″ wide
Brick Red	16 squares – 5″ 4 strips – 7½″ wide
Olive	4 strips – 3½″ wide
Gold	4 squares – 3½″ 4 squares – 7½″
Rust	4 squares – 5″ 4 squares – 3½″
Binding	9 strips 2½″ wide

Directions

Use ¼″ seam allowance unless otherwise noted.

1. Nine-patch blocks:

   a. Make 2 strip sets as shown with purple strips on each side and teal strips in center.

   b. Cut remaining strips for nine-patch blocks into four segments of approximately 10″ each. Make one 10″ strip set with teal strips on each side and black in the center. Repeat with gold, brick, and olive centers. Press.

   c. Crosscut all strip sets into 2″ segments.

   d. Make four nine-patch blocks as shown with black centers, four with gold centers, four with brick centers, and four with olive centers.

2. Stitch nine-patch blocks into 3 rows alternating with 5″ brick red and rust squares. See diagram. Stitch rows together. Press.

3. Stitch blocks from Step 2 into 3 rows alternating with 14″ black squares. Stitch rows together. Press.

4. Border 1: Measure width of quilt. Cut four 3½″ olive strips to the measured length and stitch

two to opposite sides of quilt. Stitch 3½″ gold squares to each end of remaining two olive strips and stitch one to top and one to bottom. Press.

5. Cut 33¾″ squares in half diagonally. Stitch one to each side of quilt. Press.

6. Border 2: Stitch 3½″ teal border strips end to end and then repeat Step 4, adding 3½″ rust squares to ends of teal borders put on last.

7. Border 3: Repeat Step 6 using 7½″ black and brick border strips and 7½″ gold squares. Place black on opposite sides and brick red on opposite sides.

8. Piece backing to same size as batting. Layer and quilt as desired. Trim backing and batting even with top.

9. Stitch binding strips end to end. Press in half lengthwise, wrong sides together. Bind quilt using ⅜″ seam allowance.

1a. 1b.

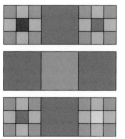

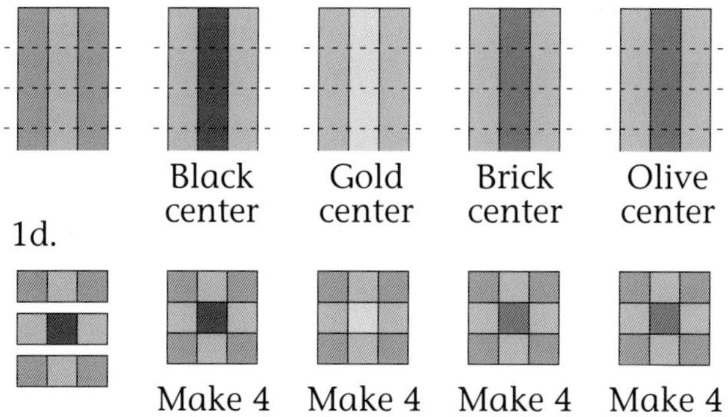

Black center   Gold center   Brick center   Olive center

1d.

Make 4   Make 4   Make 4   Make 4

2.

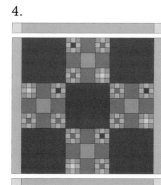

Make 4

3.

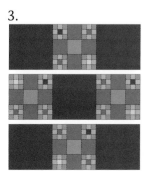

4.

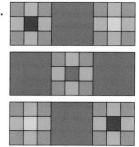

Amish Pillow

Photo on page 57. 19-20″ square.

Use 42-44″-wide fabric. When strips appear in the cutting list, cut crossgrain strips (selvage to selvage).

Materials   Solids or mottled solids

Black – incl. backing	1⅛ yds.
Purple, teal	⅛ yd. each
Brick red	¼ yd.
Gold	¼ yd.
Pillow form	20″

Cutting

Black	2 squares – 2″
	2 strips – 3¼″ wide
	2 rectangles – 19½×28″
Purple, teal	20 squares each – 2″
Brick red	1 square – 2″
	4 squares – 5″
Gold	2 squares – 2″
	4 squares – 3¼″

Directions

Use ¼″ seam allowance unless otherwise noted.

1. Make nine-patches with 2″ squares as shown.

2. Stitch nine-patches into 3 rows, alternating with 5″ brick red squares. Stitch rows together. Press pillow top.

3. Border: Measure width of pillow top. From 3¼″ black strip, cut four pieces to the measured length and stitch two to opposite sides of pillow top. Stitch 3¼″ gold squares to ends of remaining two black border strips. Stitch to other sides of pillow top. Press.

4. Press 19½×28″ rectangles in half, wrong sides together, to 19½×14″. Place both pieces on right side of pillow top, matching raw edges and overlapping folded edges in center. Stitch around entire outside edge. Clip corners, turn right side out. Insert pillow form.

1.

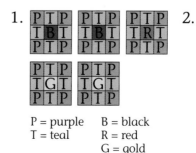

P = purple   B = black
T = teal   R = red
             G = gold

2.

59

Peace & Plenty Door Topper, Witch Door Topper, Welcome Door Topper **61**
See Photo Index on Page 3

Bear Tracks

Photos on pages 53, 60

Approximate size 53x70″

10½″ blocks set on point with 1½″ sashing

Use 42-44″-wide fabric. When strips appear in the cutting list, cut crossgrain strips (selvage to selvage).

Yardage

Background	4⅜ yds.
Bear's Paws	⅙ yd. each of 12 fabrics
"Chain"	1⅛ yds.
Backing	3½ yds.
Binding	⅝ yd.
Batting	59x76″

Cutting

Bear's Paw Blocks

Background	48 rectangles – 2x5″
	48 squares – 2″
	96 squares – 2⅜″
Each block fabric	4 squares – 3½″
	1 square – 2″
	8 squares – 2⅜″

"Chain" Blocks

Background	6 strips – 2″ wide
	4 strips – 3½″ wide
	4 strips – 5″ wide
	2 strips – 8″ wide
"Chain"	13 strips – 2″ wide

Sashing

Background	76 rectangles – 2x11″
"Chain"	31 squares – 2″
Binding	7 strips 2½″ wide

Directions

Use ¼″ seam allowance unless otherwise noted.

1. Bear's Paw blocks: Make 12 blocks following Steps 1-2 and diagrams on page 71. Press.

2. "Chain" blocks:
   a. Make 2 strip sets each A, B, and C, and 1 strip set D as shown.
   b. Crosscut strip sets into 2″ segments.
   c. Make 20 blocks with segments as shown. Press.

3. Stitch diagonal rows of Bear's Paw and "Chain" blocks together with sashing rectangles. Stitch rows of sashing rectangles and "chain" squares together. See diagram.

4. Stitch rows of blocks and rows of sashing together. Press.

5. Trim edge of quilt ⅜″ outside corners of "chain" squares as shown.

6. Piece backing horizontally to same size as batting. Layer and quilt as desired. Trim backing and batting even with top.

7. Stitch binding strips end to end. Press in half lengthwise, wrong sides together. Bind quilt using ⅜″ seam allowance.

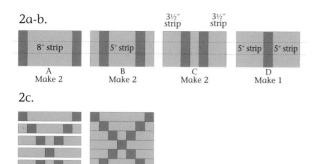

2a-b.

A	B	C	D
8″ strip	5″ strip	3½″ strip / 3½″ strip	5″ strip / 5″ strip
Make 2	Make 2	Make 2	Make 1

2c.

3-4.

5.

Bear Tracks Pillow

Photo on page 60.   13-14″ square.

Use 42-44″-wide fabric. When strips appear in the cutting list, cut crossgrain strips (selvage to selvage).

Materials

Background	⅓ yd.
Bear's Paw	⅙ yd.
Corner setting squares	⅛ yd.
Backing	½ yd.
Pillow form	14″

Cutting

Background	4 rectangles – 2x5″
	4 squares – 2″
	8 squares – 2⅜″
	4 rectangles – 2x11″
Bear's Paw fabric	4 squares – 3½″
	1 square – 2″
	8 squares – 2⅜″
Corner setting squares	4 squares – 2″
Backing	2 rectangles – 14x20″

Directions

Use ¼″ seam allowance unless otherwise noted.

1. Make Bear's Paw block following Steps 1-2 and diagrams on page 71. Press.

2. Stitch two 2x11″ rectangles to opposite sides of block. Stitch corner setting squares to each end of remaining 2x11″ rectangles. Stitch to remaining sides of block. Press.

3. Press 14x20″ rectangles in half, wrong sides together, to 14x10″. Place both pieces on right side of pillow top, matching raw edges and overlapping folded edges in center. Stitch around entire outside edge. Clip corners, turn right side out. Insert pillow form.

2.

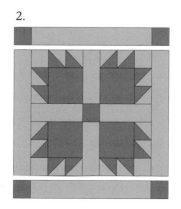

63

Spooky Friends Place Mats, Harvest Scarecrow, Cookie Caddy, Plate Charmers, Pumpkins
See Photo Index on Page 3

Crayon Frameups

Photo on page 20

17-18″ pillow

9x12″ or 11x14″ framed pictures

Use 42-44″-wide fabric.

Materials

Background	½ yd.
Muslin for presscloth	⅜ yd.
Freezer paper	12x15″
Good-quality crayons	
Fine permanent marking pen	black
Buttons for eyes – optional	⅝″
Borders for pillow	⅛ yd. each of 10 fabrics
Backing for pillow	¾ yd.
Pillow form	18″
Picture frame & hardware	9x12″ or 11x14″
Matboard for 11x14″ picture	11x14″ with 8x11″ opening

Foamcore for framed picture

Coloring Directions

Patterns on pages 83-85.

Note: Make a practice piece to be sure the chosen crayon colors are dark enough. It's also a good idea to do a heat-set and washing test.

1. Wash and iron background fabric. Cut a rectangle 14x17″.

2. Press shiny side of freezer paper to wrong side of fabric rectangle. Photocopy pattern.

3. Center photocopy right side down on freezer paper side of fabric. Tape in place. Using a light box or a window, trace design on fabric with permanent marker.

4. Fill in design areas with crayon. Remove freezer paper.

5. Protect ironing board with paper or muslin. Lay fabric with colored design right side up on ironing board. Lay a piece of muslin on top. Preheat iron to medium-hot (cotton). Heat-set design for several seconds.

Pillow Directions

Use ¼″ seam allowance unless otherwise noted.

1. Cut a 2″ strip from each border fabric.

2. Cut crayon rectangle to 9x12″. Stitch 2″ strips to right side of rectangle first, then bottom, then left side, then top. Trim ends of strips as you go. Repeat for one more round. Add additional strips to each side. See diagram. Press.

3. Cut 2 backing pieces 24x18″. Press each in half, wrong sides together, to 12x18″. Place both pieces on right side of pillow top, matching raw edges and overlapping folded edges in center. Stitch around entire outside edge. Clip corners, turn right side out. Insert pillow form.

Framed Picture Directions

1. Cut foamcore to fit frame. Wrap colored picture around foamcore and tape edges. Check alignment with matboard opening if using 11x14″ frame.

2. Place in frame and secure with hardware.

3. Cover back with brown wrapping paper if desired.

Spooky Friends
Place Mats & Wall Hanging

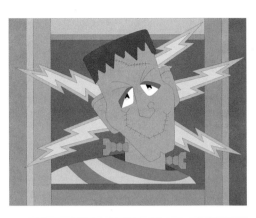

Place Mats 13x17″

Photo on page 64

Use 42-44″-wide fabric. When strips appear in the cutting list, cut crossgrain strips (selvage to selvage).

Yardage Makes 1

Background	½ yd.
Borders	scraps up to 3x14″
Appliques	scraps up to 10x12″
Backing	½ yd.
Binding	¼ yd.
Thin cotton batting	16x20″
Fusible web	1½-2 yds.

Cutting Patterns on pages 35-37, 78, 91-98

Background	13½x17½″
Appliques	use photo & diagram as guides
Backing	16x20″
Binding	2 strips 2½″ wide

Directions

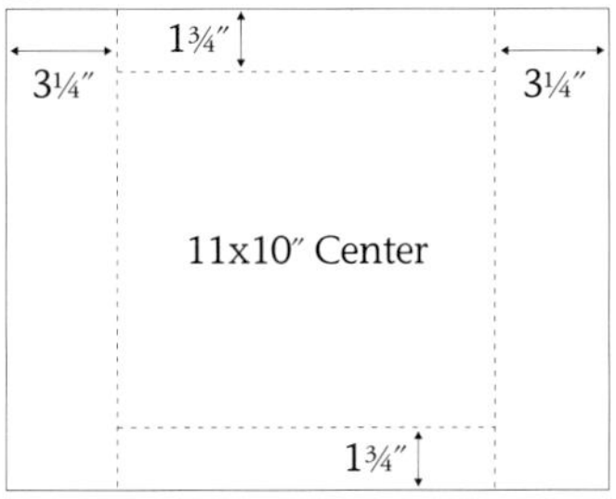

1. Mark vertical and horizontal lines lightly on right side of background rectangle as shown.

2. Trace appliques to fusible web adding "underlap" where needed. Fuse to desired fabrics and cut out. Set aside.

   1.

   3¼″   1¾″   3¼″

   11x10″ Center

   1¾″

3. Borders

   a. Fuse web to wrong sides of strips of fabric bigger than the following cut sizes for borders, then cut out borders:

      2 for top & bottom – ⅜x11½″
      2 for top & bottom – 1¾x11½″
      2 for sides – ½x13½″
      4 for sides – 1⅝x13½″

   b. Top & bottom: Lay 1¾x11½″ pieces right side up on ironing board. Peel paper from ⅜x11½″ pieces and place them on 1¾x11½″ pieces, right side up, as shown. Fuse.

      3b. Top & Bottom

   c. Sides: Lay two 1⅝x13½″ pieces, right side up, long cut edges meeting, on ironing board. Peel paper from a

      3c. Sides

½ x13½" piece and place on 1⅝x13½" pieces, right side up, centered, as shown. See diagram. Fuse. Repeat for other side.

4. Peel backing from all border and applique pieces. Layer pieces on background rectangle using photo, diagram, and the following directions as guides. Fuse once all pieces are in place. Note: Side border units should overlap ends of top and bottom units.

Frankenstein's shirt should be covered slightly by borders. Lightening bolts go under head but on top of borders.

Dracula's shirt should be covered slightly by bottom border, and his hand should be placed on top of border.

Witch's neck, hat top, and web should be covered slightly by borders. Hair and right side of hat brim should overlap borders. Push hair pieces as far up under hat as needed to match photo and diagram.

Princess's dress, sleeves, hand, and hair should be covered slightly by the borders. Crown, frog, and pinkie finger should overlap borders.

5. Stitch edges of appliques and borders with machine zigzag or buttonhole stitch.

6. Lay backing rectangle wrong side up on table. Lay batting on backing. Center place mat right side up on batting. Quilt as desired. Trim backing and batting even with top.

7. Stitch binding strips end to end. Press in half lengthwise, wrong sides together. Bind place mat using ⅜" seam allowance.

Wall Hanging Approximate size 18x63"

Photo on back cover

Use 42-44"-wide fabric. When strips appear in the cutting list, cut crossgrain strips (selvage to selvage).

Yardage

Background	⅓ yd. each of 4 fabrics
Block borders, & applique	see page 66
Sashing	¼ yd.
Border 1	⅙ yd.
Border 2	½ yd.
Backing	1½ yds.
Binding	½ yd.
Batting	22x67"
Fusible web	6 yds.

Cutting Patterns on pages 35-37, 78, 91-98

Background		4 rectangles 11½ x10½"
Sashing		3 rectangles 2½x14"
Block borders	top & bottom	8 rectangles ⅞x11½"
	top & bottom	8 rectangles 1⅝x11½"
	sides	8 rectangles 1¾x13½"

Continued on page 99.

Door Toppers

Photos on pages 32, 61

Approximate size 9x30″

Use 42-44″-wide fabric.

Materials

Background	½ yd.
Lower section of Welcome	¼ yd.
Appliques	scraps up to 12x12″
Muslin – quilting & backing	1 yd.
Binding	⅓ yd.
Batting	14x34″
Poster board	1 piece

Cutting
Patterns on pages 35, 46, 72, 73, 80, 86-92

Background	1 rectangle – 14x34″
Lower section of Welcome	1 rectangle – 4½x34″
Appliques	use photo & diagram as guides
Muslin	2 rectangles – 14x34″
Binding	**bias** strips 2½″ wide to make 80″-long piece
Poster board	use dashed line indicated on pattern piece

Directions

1. Make full-sized background arch pattern (page 88). Cut out pattern on outside line. Lay pattern on right side of background rectangle and draw a line around it to use as a design-area guide.

2. Applique using your favorite method. Our favorite method is fusible web, and our patterns are set up for it—reversed for tracing and no seam allowances added. Keep appliques ¾″ from curved edge except for witch and web.

3. Layer appliqued piece with batting and one of the muslin rectangles. Quilt as desired. Cut out on line drawn in Step 1.

4. Cut out a muslin backing using quilted piece as a pattern. Hem bottom of muslin arch with a ¾″ single-fold hem.

Welcome

Trick or Treat

Peace & Plenty

5. Baste hemmed muslin and quilted piece, wrong sides together, along curved edge, leaving hemmed edge free.

6. Stitch binding strips together end to end. Cut off a piece 34″ long. Fold in half wrong sides together and stitch to right side of bottom edge of Door Topper with a ⅜″ seam allowance. Trim raw ends even with Topper. Hand stitch to back at seamline. Bind curved edge with remaining binding, folding in raw ends at corners.

7. Slide poster board into pocket. Trim if necessary to make fit.

8. Blind hem bottom edge of muslin to backing of quilted piece or tack at intervals.

9. Hang on wall above door with fine straight pins.

Autumn Table Runner

Photo on page 52.   Approximate size 14x66″.   7″ blocks set on point.

Use 42-44″-wide fabric. When strips appear in the cutting list, cut cross-grain strips (selvage to selvage).

Yardage

Block background	⅜ yd.	Border 1	¼ yd.
Bear's Paws	½ yd.	Border 2	½ yd.
Setting triangles	⅝ yd.	Backing	1¼ yds.
Appliques	scraps up to 5x7″	Binding	½ yd.
		Batting	18x70″

Cutting Patterns on pages 44, 77, 80, 82

Block background	20 rectangles – 1½x3½″
	20 squares – 1½″
	40 squares – 1⅞″ – cut in half diagonally
Bear's Paws	20 squares – 2½″
	5 squares – 1½″
	40 squares – 1⅞″ – cut in half diagonally
Setting triangles	3 squares – 11¼″ – cut in quarters diagonally (A)
	2 squares – 5⅞″ – cut in half diagonally (B)
Appliques	leaves: 20 large, 2 medium, 2 small – 20 acorns – 24 berries – 2 baskets – 6 apples
Border 1	4 strips 1″ wide
Border 2	5 strips 2¼″ wide
Binding	5 strips 2½″ wide

Directions

1. Make blocks using diagrams on page 71. Press. Stitch blocks and A and B triangles into diagonal rows as shown. Stitch rows together. Stitch A triangles to ends.

2. Borders: Stitch Border 1 strips to the diagonal ends of quilt. Trim excess. Measure sides of quilt. Piece border strips to the measured length and stitch to sides of quilt. Repeat with Border 2 strips.

Continued on page 86.

Autumn Sampler

Photo on page 20

Approximate size 52x68″

8″ blocks set 5x7

Use 42-44″-wide fabric. When strips appear in the cutting list, cut crossgrain strips (selvage to selvage).

Yardage

Blocks	¼ yd. each of 15-25 lights, mediums, & darks
Border 1	½ yd.
Border 2	1 yd.
Backing	3½ yds.
Binding	⅔ yd.
Batting	58x74″

Cutting

Mix lights, mediums & darks as desired.

Block A	320 squares – 2½″
Block B	8 squares – 4½″
	32 squares – 2½″
	64 squares – 2⅞″
Block C	7 squares – 4½″
	14 squares – 3¾″
	14 squares – 4⅞″
Border 1	5 strips 2½″ wide
Border 2	6 strips 4½″ wide
Binding	7 strips 2½″ wide

Directions

1. Cut all 2⅞″, 3¾″, and 4⅞″ squares in half diagonally.

2. Make 20 Block A, 8 Block B, and 7 Block C referring to diagrams. Press.

3. Stitch blocks into 7 rows of 5 blocks as shown in whole-quilt diagram. Stitch rows together. Press.

4. Border 1: Measure length of quilt. Piece border strips to the measured length and stitch to sides of quilt. Repeat at top and bottom. Press.

5. Border 2: Repeat Step 4.

6. Piece backing horizontally to same size as batting. Layer and quilt as desired. Trim backing and batting even with top.

7. Stitch binding strips end to end. Press in half lengthwise, wrong sides together. Bind quilt using ⅜″ seam allowance.

2.

For 1 Block A

For 1 Block B

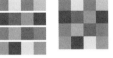

Make 8

Make 4

For 1 Block C

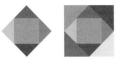

70

Harvest Glow

Photo on front cover

Approximate size 51x61″

10½″ blocks set 4x5

Use 42-44″-wide fabric. When strips appear in the cutting list, cut crossgrain strips (selvage to selvage).

Yardage

Background & borders – black   2¾ yds.
Block fabrics   ⅝ yd. each of 4
Backing   3½ yds.
Binding   ⅝ yd.
Batting   57x67″

Cutting

Background
    Blocks   80 squares – 2″
                  80 rectangles – 2x5″
                  160 squares – 2⅜″
    Borders 1 & 3   11 strips 2″ wide
    Border 2   67 squares – 2⅜″
                  4 squares – 2″

Each block fabric
    Blocks   20 squares – 3½″
                  5 squares – 2″
                  40 squares – 2⅜″
    Border 2   17 squares of each fabric– 2⅜″
Binding   6 strips 2½″ wide

Directions

1. Cut all 2⅜″ squares in half diagonally.

2. Make 5 blocks with each block fabric, referring to diagrams. Press.

3. Stitch blocks into 5 rows of 4. Stitch rows together. Press.

4. Border 1: Measure length of quilt. Piece border strips to the measured length and stitch to sides of quilt. Repeat at top and bottom. Press.

5. Border 2: Make 134 half-square triangle units with remaining triangles cut from 2⅜″ squares. Stitch units into 2 side borders of 30 units each and 2 top/bottom borders of 37 units each. See diagram. Note changes of direction at asterisks. Stitch 2″ background squares to each end of top and bottom borders. Stitch side borders to

2.
For One Block

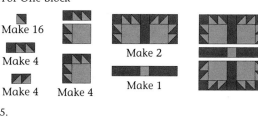

Make 16

Make 4

Make 4   Make 4

Make 2

Make 1

5.
Make 2 for Sides

Make 2 for Top & Bottom

quilt first, then top and bottom borders. Press.

6. Border 3: Repeat Step 4.

7. Piece backing horizontally to same size as batting. Layer and quilt as desired. Trim backing and batting even with top.

8. Stitch binding strips end to end. Press in half lengthwise, wrong sides together. Bind quilt using ⅜″ seam allowance.

Trick or Treat
Witch Door Topper

Place tail
behind branch

Use permanent
marker for eyes

Patterns are
reversed for tracing
to fusible web

72

Trick or Treat
Witch Door Topper

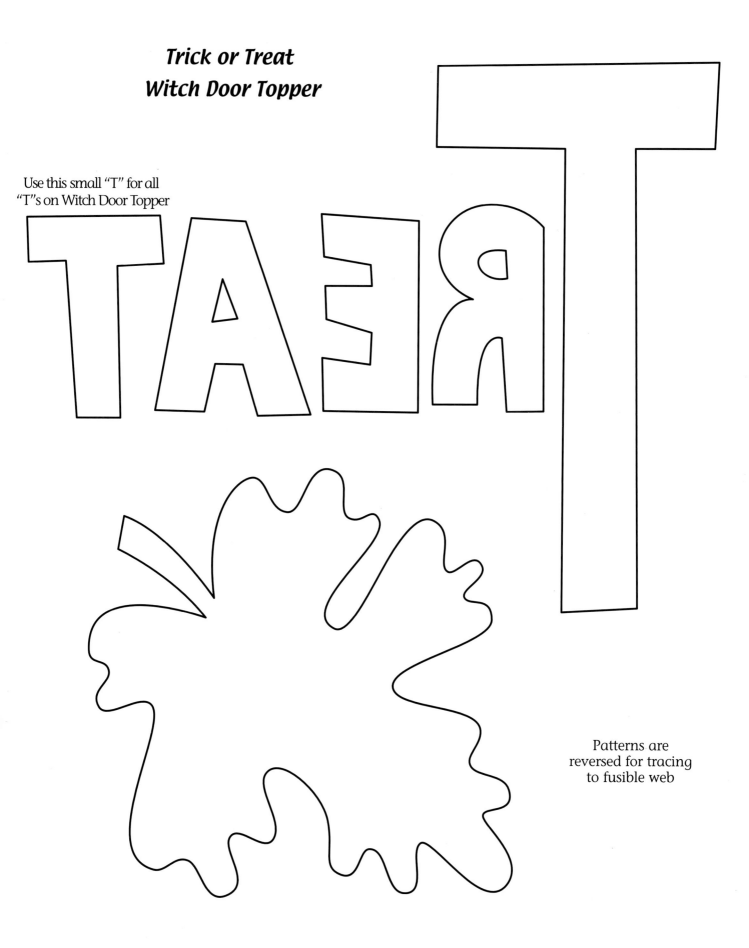

Use this small "T" for all
"T"s on Witch Door Topper

Patterns are
reversed for tracing
to fusible web

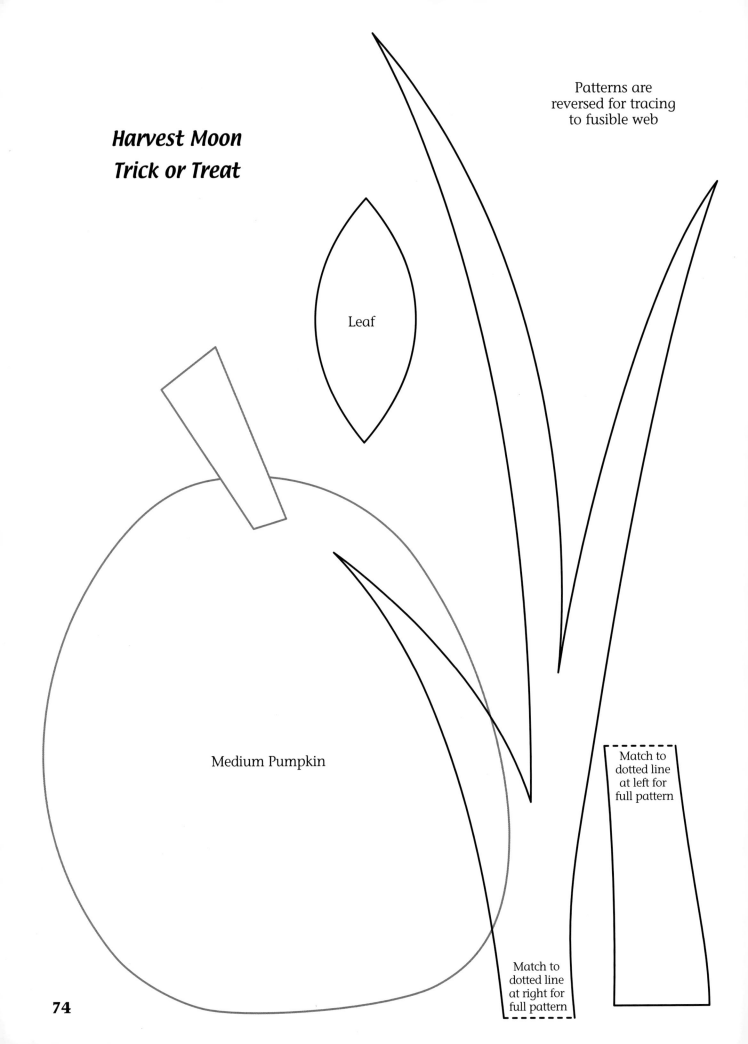

Harvest Moon
Trick or Treat

Patterns are
reversed for tracing
to fusible web

Leaf

Medium Pumpkin

Match to
dotted line
at left for
full pattern

Match to
dotted line
at right for
full pattern

74

Small Pumpkin/Jack-o'-lantern

Patterns are
reversed for tracing
to fusible web

Large Pumpkin/Jack-o'-lantern

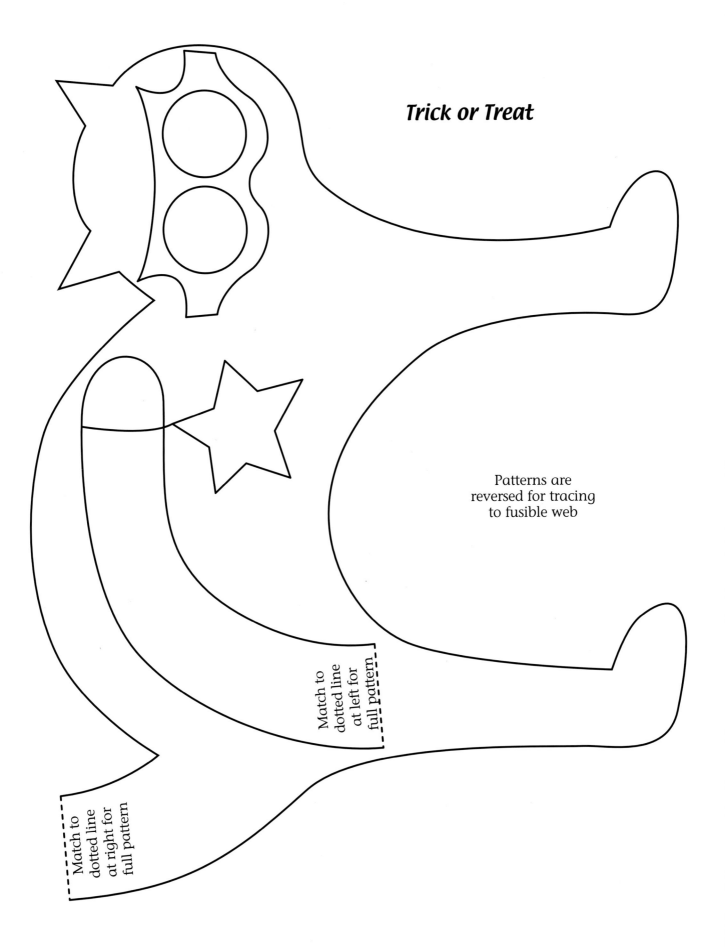

Trick or Treat

Patterns are
reversed for tracing
to fusible web

Match to
dotted line
at left for
full pattern

Match to
dotted line
at right for
full pattern

Harvest Moon
Trick or Treat
Autumn Table Runner

Patterns are
reversed for tracing
to fusible web

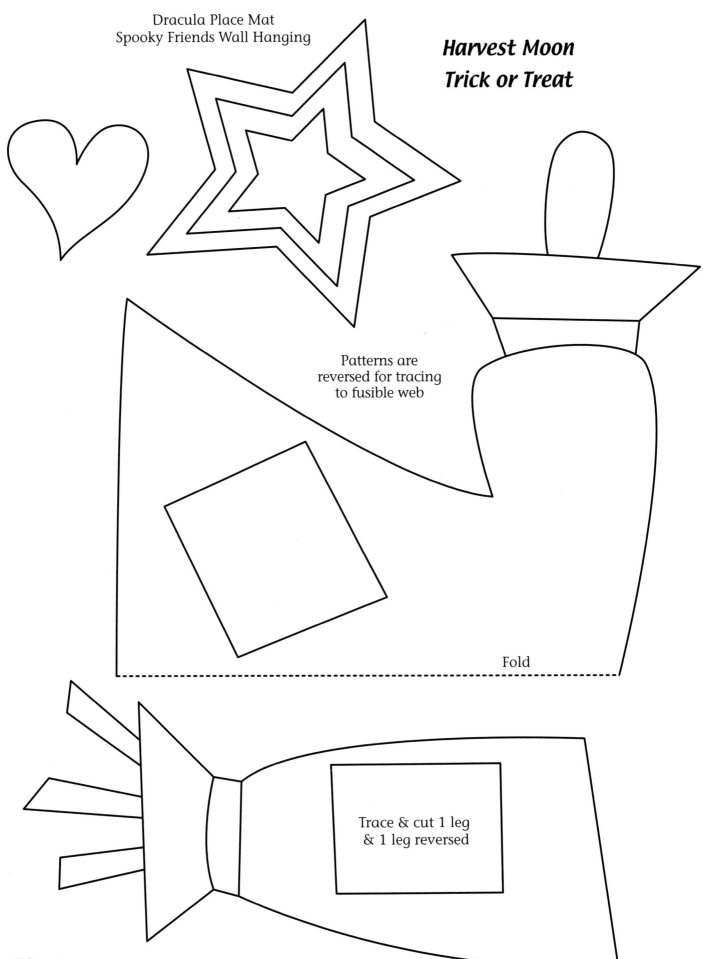

Dracula Place Mat
Spooky Friends Wall Hanging

Harvest Moon
Trick or Treat

Patterns are
reversed for tracing
to fusible web

Fold

Trace & cut 1 leg
& 1 leg reversed

Harvest Moon

Use permanent marker for eyes

Patterns are reversed for tracing to fusible web

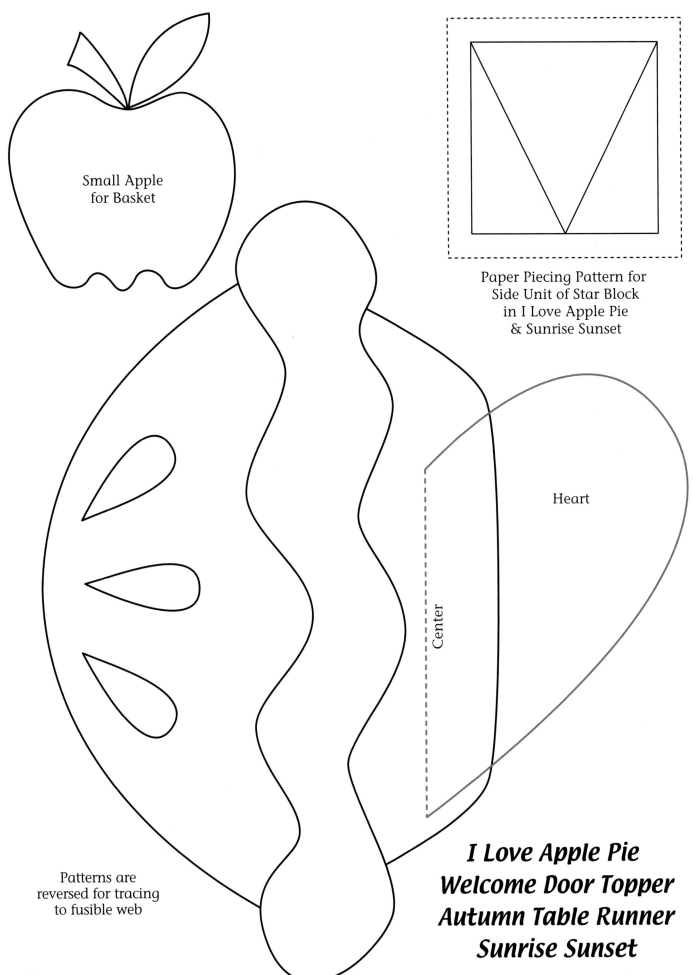

Small Apple
for Basket

Paper Piecing Pattern for
Side Unit of Star Block
in I Love Apple Pie
& Sunrise Sunset

Heart

Center

Patterns are
reversed for tracing
to fusible web

*I Love Apple Pie
Welcome Door Topper
Autumn Table Runner
Sunrise Sunset*

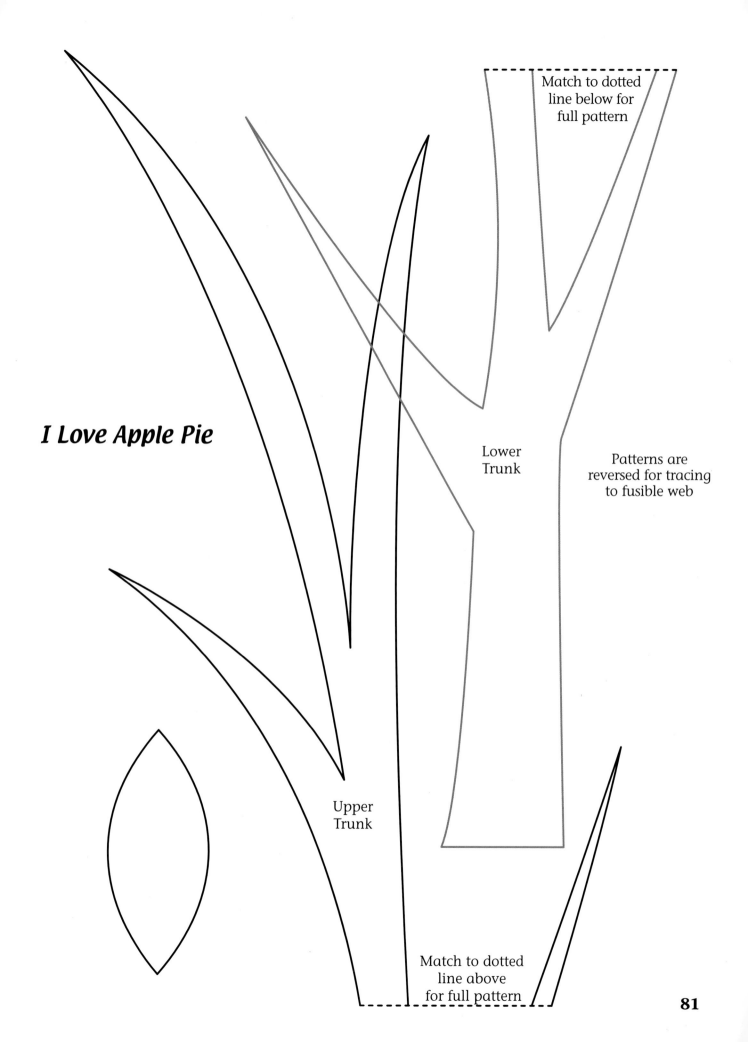

I Love Apple Pie

Match to dotted
line below for
full pattern

Lower
Trunk

Patterns are
reversed for tracing
to fusible web

Upper
Trunk

Match to dotted
line above
for full pattern

81

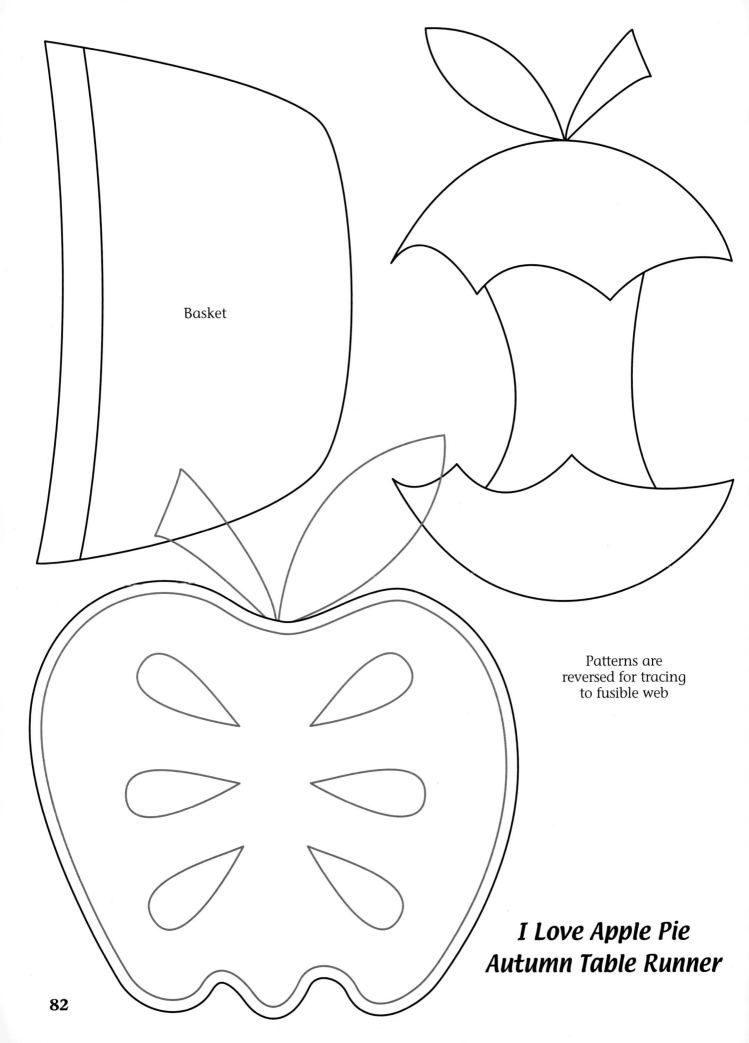

Basket

Patterns are
reversed for tracing
to fusible web

**I Love Apple Pie
Autumn Table Runner**

82

Tricks or treats!

Crayon Frameups

Happy Halloween!

come one, come all....

Fall. is here for Fall.

Jack o' Lantern

Crayon Frameups

Happy Thanksgiving

welcome family and friends ....celebrate

heritage and harvest....give.

thanks the good earth has blessed us all.

Autumn treasures

of crispy breezes and

freezes

Happy   Fall

before it

crunchy leaves...

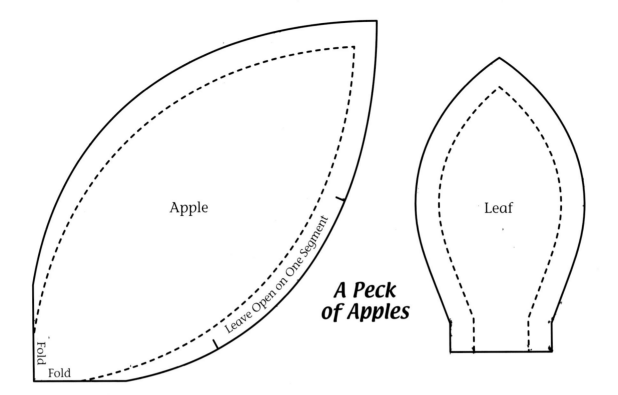

Apple

Fold

Fold

Leave Open on One Segment

Leaf

A Peck of Apples

Welcome Door Topper
Schoolhouse Plaid

Patterns are
reversed for tracing
to fusible web

Autumn Table Runner

Continued from page 69.

3. Applique using your favorite
   method. Our favorite method
   is fusible web, and our patterns are set up for it—
   reversed for tracing and no
   seam allowances added.

4. Piece backing to same size as
   batting. Layer top with backing and batting. Quilt as
   desired. Trim backing and
   batting even with top.

5. Stitch binding strips together
   end to end. Press in half
   lengthwise, wrong sides
   together. Bind quilt using ⅜″
   seam allowance.

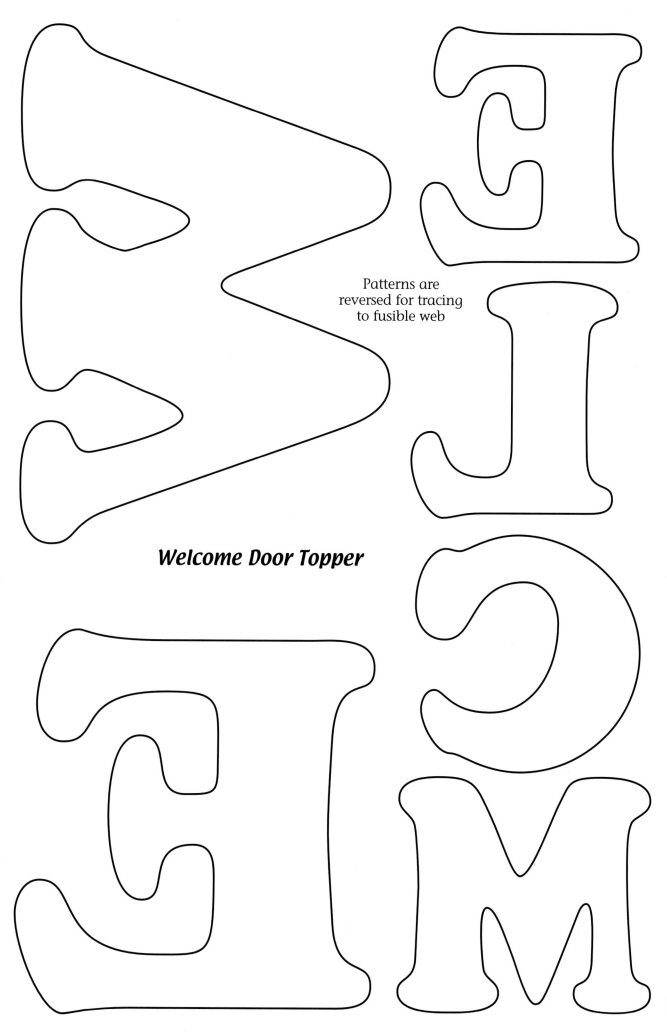

Patterns are
reversed for tracing
to fusible web

Welcome Door Topper

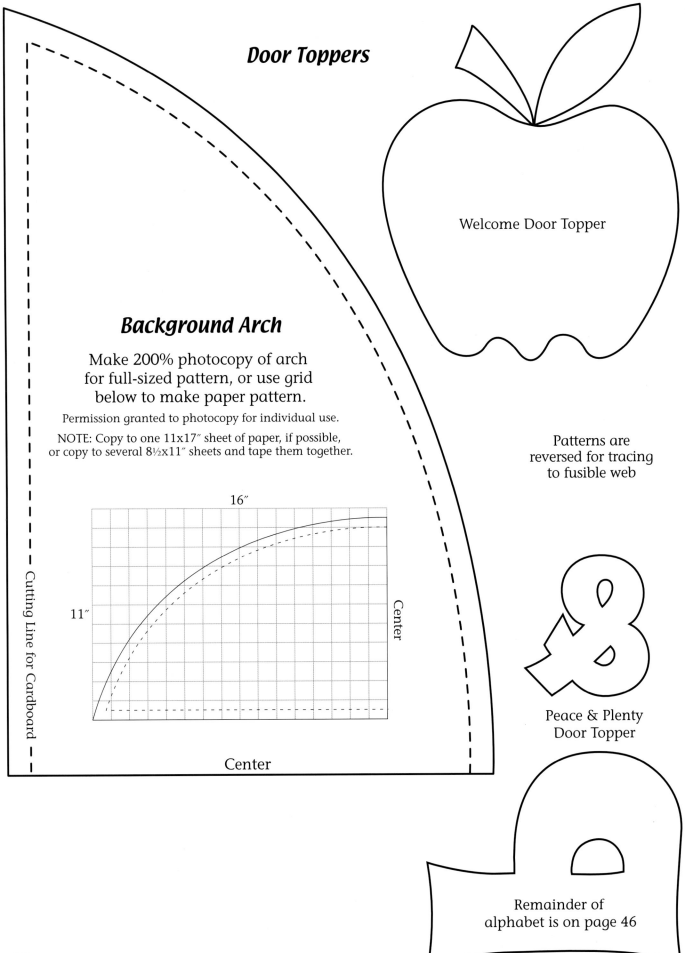

Door Toppers

Welcome Door Topper

Background Arch

Make 200% photocopy of arch for full-sized pattern, or use grid below to make paper pattern.

Permission granted to photocopy for individual use.

NOTE: Copy to one 11x17" sheet of paper, if possible, or copy to several 8½x11" sheets and tape them together.

16"

11"

Center

Center

Cutting Line for Cardboard

Patterns are reversed for tracing to fusible web

Peace & Plenty Door Topper

Remainder of alphabet is on page 46

Door Toppers

Witch Door Topper

Witch Door Topper

Peace & Plenty Door Topper

Patterns are reversed for tracing to fusible web

Match to dotted line on top of page 90 for full pattern

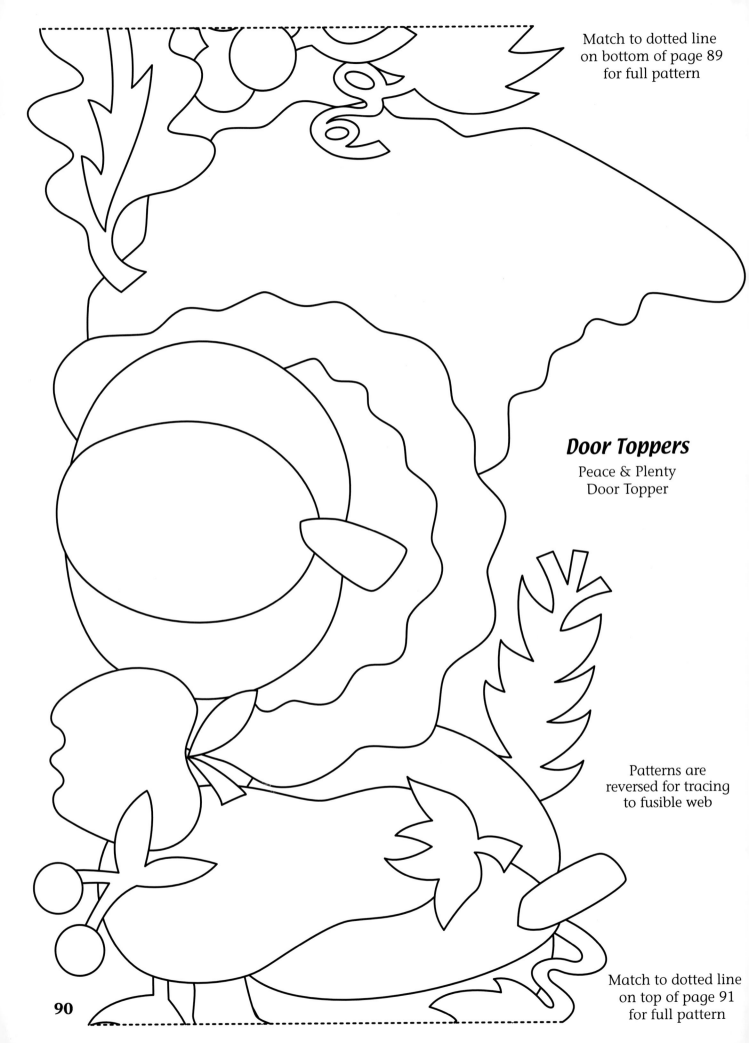

Match to dotted line
on bottom of page 89
for full pattern

Door Toppers
Peace & Plenty
Door Topper

Patterns are
reversed for tracing
to fusible web

Match to dotted line
on top of page 91
for full pattern

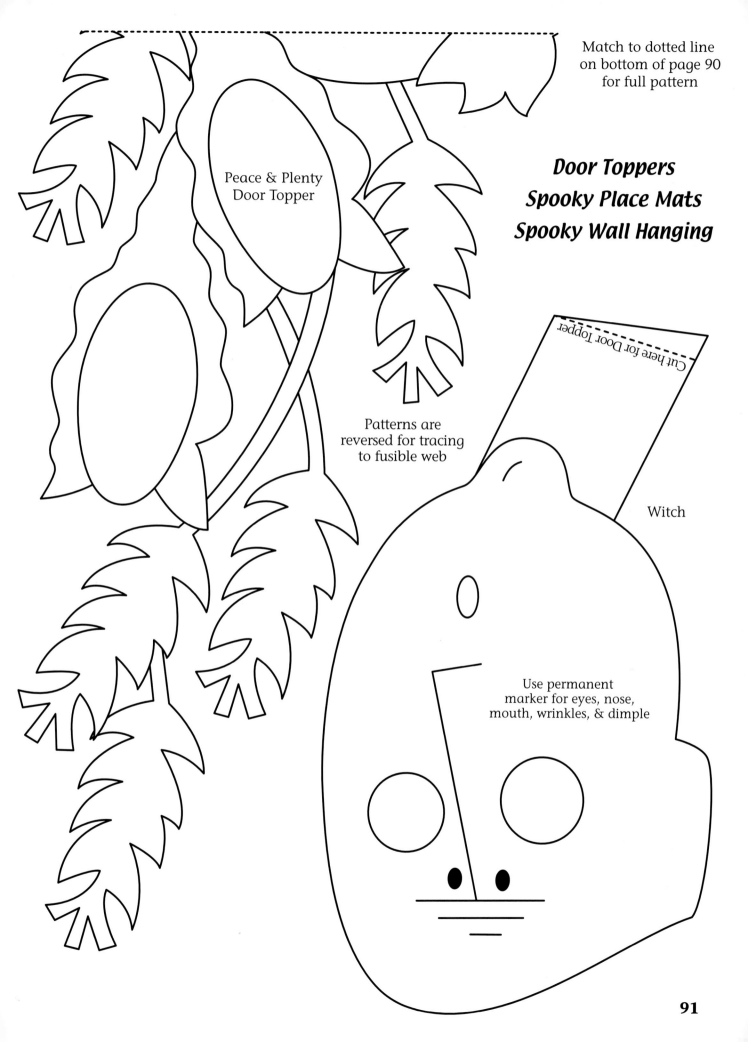

Match to dotted line
on bottom of page 90
for full pattern

**Door Toppers
Spooky Place Mats
Spooky Wall Hanging**

Peace & Plenty
Door Topper

Patterns are
reversed for tracing
to fusible web

Cut here for Door Topper

Witch

Use permanent
marker for eyes, nose,
mouth, wrinkles, & dimple

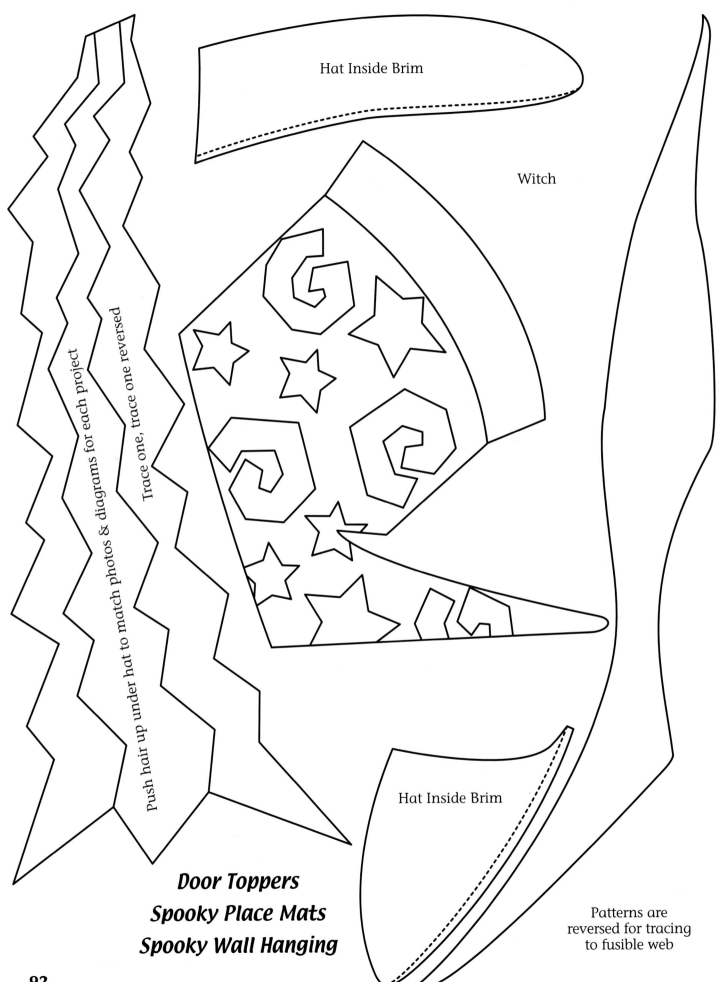

Hat Inside Brim

Witch

Trace one, trace one reversed

Push hair up under hat to match photos & diagrams for each project

Hat Inside Brim

**Door Toppers
Spooky Place Mats
Spooky Wall Hanging**

Patterns are
reversed for tracing
to fusible web

92

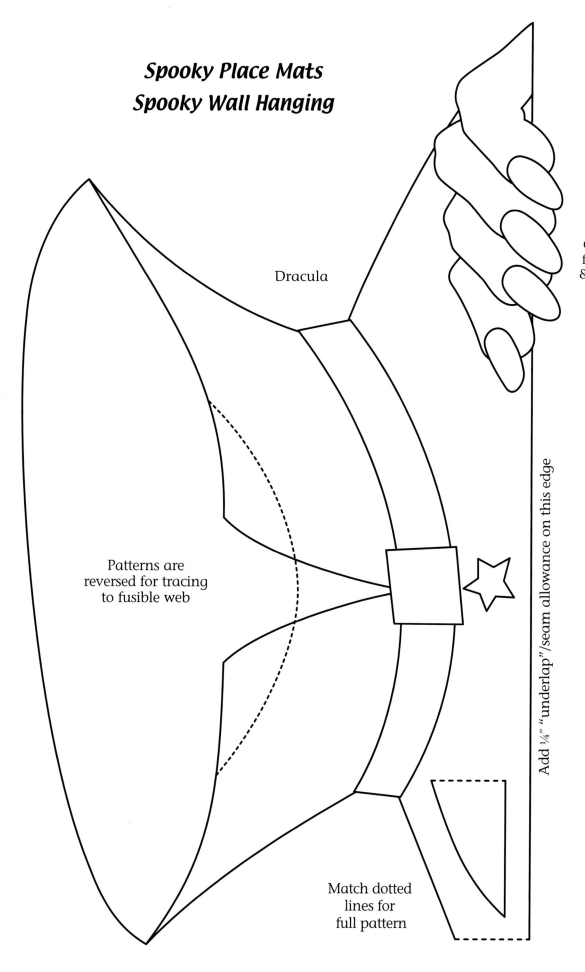

Spooky Place Mats
Spooky Wall Hanging

Dracula

Cut one piece of
fabric for fingers
& use permanent
marker for lines
between fingers

Patterns are
reversed for tracing
to fusible web

Add ¼" "underlap"/seam allowance on this edge

Match dotted
lines for
full pattern

Spooky Place Mats
Spooky Wall Hanging

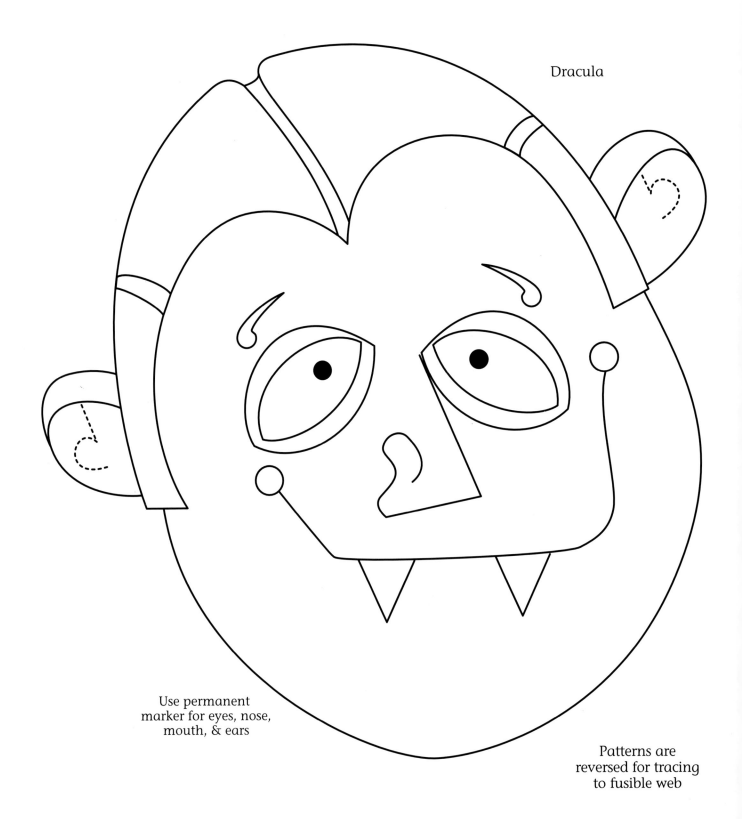

Dracula

Use permanent marker for eyes, nose, mouth, & ears

Patterns are reversed for tracing to fusible web

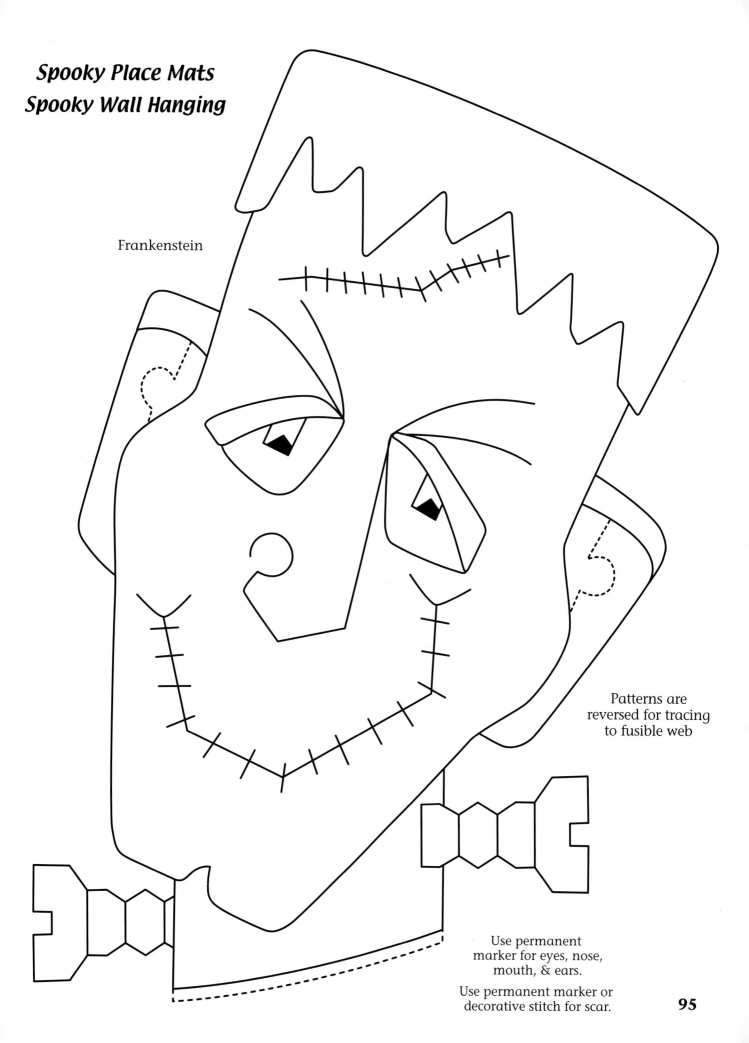

Spooky Place Mats
Spooky Wall Hanging

Frankenstein

Patterns are
reversed for tracing
to fusible web

Use permanent
marker for eyes, nose,
mouth, & ears.

Use permanent marker or
decorative stitch for scar.

Spooky Place Mats
Spooky Wall Hanging

Frankenstein

Patterns are
reversed for tracing
to fusible web

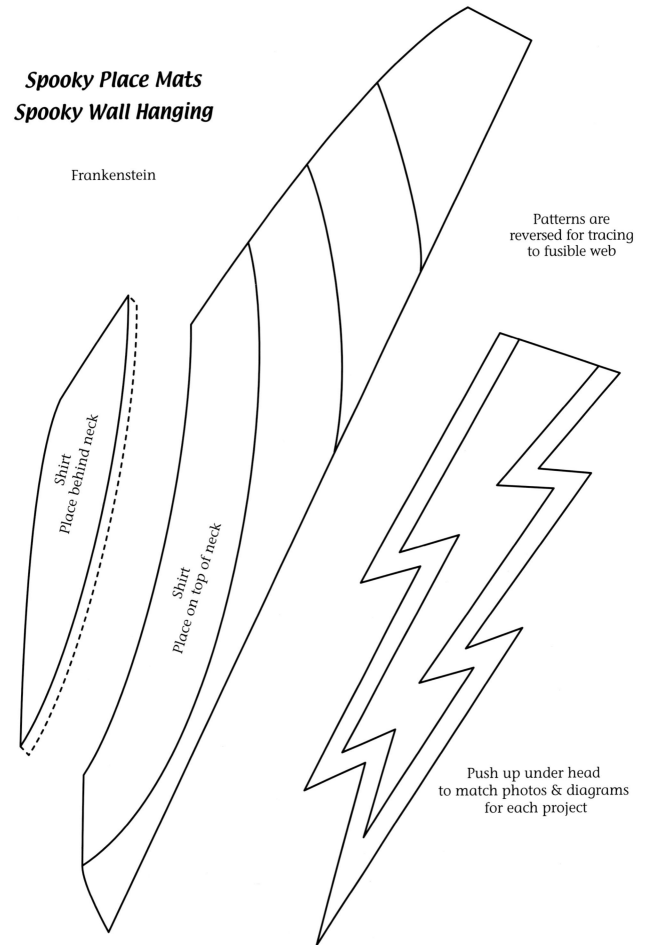

Shirt
Place behind neck

Shirt
Place on top of neck

Push up under head
to match photos & diagrams
for each project

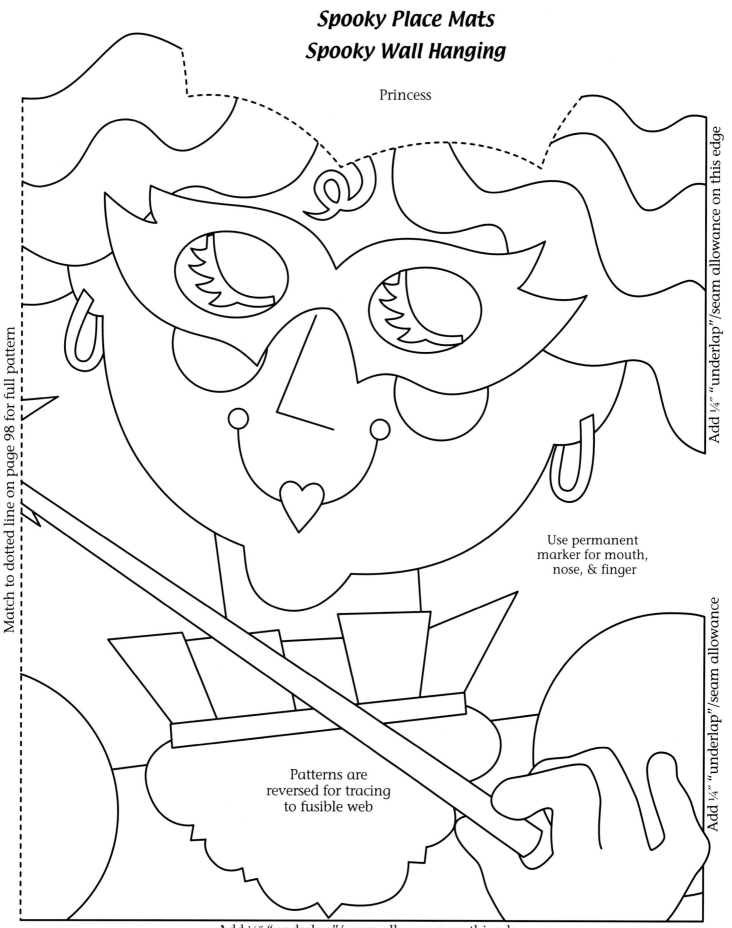

Princess

Add ¼″ "underlap"/seam allowance on this edge

Match to dotted line on page 98 for full pattern

Use permanent
marker for mouth,
nose, & finger

Add ¼″ "underlap"/seam allowance

Patterns are
reversed for tracing
to fusible web

Add ¼″ "underlap"/seam allowance on this edge

Spooky Place Mats
Spooky Wall Hanging

Princess

Add ¼" "underlap"/seam allowance on this edge

Match to dotted line on page 97 for full pattern

Patterns are
reversed for tracing
to fusible web

Spooky Friends Wall Hanging

Continued from page 67.

Border 1	4 strips 1″ wide
Border 2	4 strips 2½″ wide
Binding	5 strips 2½″ wide

Directions

1. Trace appliques to fusible web adding "underlap" where needed. Fuse to desired fabrics and cut out. Peel backing from all applique pieces. Layer pieces on background rectangles using photo and diagram as guides. Save bats, stars, Dracula's hand, spider, frog and crown for fusing **after** all borders are added. **Lightly** fuse **all but overhanging pieces** to hold temporarily in place. One inch of overhanging pieces should be left unfused around all edges of background so block borders can be added. Overhanging pieces are Witch's hair and hat brim, Frankenstein's hair and lightening bolts, and Princess' pinkie finger.

2. Stitch block borders to block background as shown. Stitch blocks together with sashing rectangles between them.

3. Border 1: Measure length of quilt. Piece border strips to the measured length and stitch to sides of quilt. Repeat at top and bottom. Press.

4. Border 2: Repeat Step 3.

5. Finish fusing the overhanging pieces, then fuse bats, stars, Dracula's hand, spider, frog, and crown.

6. Stitch appliques in place with machine zigzag or buttonhole stitch.

7. Piece backing to same size as batting. Layer and quilt as desired. Trim backing and batting even with top.

8. Stitch binding strips end to end. Press in half lengthwise, wrong sides together. Bind quilt using ⅜″ seam allowance.

2.

Appliques removed for clarity

Appliques removed for clarity

Appliques removed for clarity

Match to dotted line at bottom for full pattern

Fold

Fold

Tie Pillow

Match to dotted line at top for full pattern

Pumpkin Patch

Make 190% photocopy (or a 138%
copy of a 138% copy) for full-sized pattern.

Permission granted to photocopy for individual use.

NOTE: Copy to 11x17″ paper, if possible, or use 8½x11″ sheets and
tape them together. Always place book and subsequent copies
on copier in same direction to minimize distortion.

Patterns are
reversed for tracing
to fusible web

Fits 16x12″ block

Pumpkin Patch

Make 190% photocopy (or a 138% copy of a 138% copy) for full-sized pattern.

Permission granted to photocopy for individual use.

NOTE: Copy to 11x17″ paper, if possible, or use 8½x11″ sheets and tape them together. Always place book and subsequent copies on copier in same direction to minimize distortion.

Patterns are reversed for tracing to fusible web

These fit 8x18″ blocks

101

Pumpkin Patch

Fits 18x16″ block

Patterns are reversed for tracing to fusible web